# CYCLING THE CANAL DE LA GARONNE

## About the Author

Declan Lyons has spent many years cycling and touring in the south of France and has written a guide to cycling the Canal du Midi from Toulouse to Sète. He has travelled the routes included in this guide many times over the past two decades and the Canal de la Garonne forms part of his own regular route from the Channel to the Mediterranean. Declan is an advocate of cycle touring – taking time on his cycles and relishing the nature, history and daily life all around. He has toured the region between the Atlantic and the Mediterranean extensively by bike and packs much of what he has learnt into his guides.

### Other Cicerone guides by the author
*Cycling the Canal du Midi from Toulouse to Sète*

# CYCLING THE CANAL DE LA GARONNE

## FROM BORDEAUX TO TOULOUSE

### by Declan Lyons

JUNIPER HOUSE, MURLEY MOSS,
OXENHOLME ROAD, KENDAL, CUMBRIA LA9 7RL
www.cicerone.co.uk

© Declan Lyons 2019
First edition 2019
ISBN: 978 1 85284 783 8

Printed by KHL Printing, Singapore
A catalogue record for this book is available from the British Library.
All photographs are by the author unless otherwise stated.

Route mapping by Lovell Johns www.lovelljohns.com
Contains OpenStreetMap.org data © OpenStreetMap
contributors, CC-BY-SA. NASA relief data courtesy of ESRI

## Updates to this guide

While every effort is made by our authors to ensure the accuracy of guide-books as they go to print, changes can occur during the lifetime of an edition. Any updates that we know of for this guide will be on the Cicerone website (www.cicerone.co.uk/783/updates), so please check before planning your trip. We also advise that you check information about such things as transport, accommodation and shops locally. Even rights of way can be altered over time.

The route maps in this guide are derived from publicly available data, databases and crowd-sourced data. As such they have not been through the detailed checking procedures that would generally be applied to a published map from an official mapping agency, although naturally we have reviewed them closely in the light of local knowledge as part of the preparation of this guide.

We are always grateful for information about any discrepancies between a guidebook and the facts on the ground, sent by email to updates@cicerone.co.uk or by post to Cicerone, Juniper House, Murley Moss, Oxenholme Road, Kendal, LA9 7RL.

**Register your book:** To sign up to receive free updates, special offers and GPX files where available, register your book at www.cicerone.co.uk.

*Front cover: Moulin de Loubens (Stage 2)*

# CONTENTS

# ROUTE SUMMARY TABLE

| Stage | Start | Finish | Distance | Climb | Page |
|-------|-------|--------|----------|-------|------|
| Prologue | Bordeaux | Lacanau Océan | 135km | 220m | 46 |
| Stage 1 | Bordeaux | Sauveterre-de-Guyenne | 59.1km | 166m | 58 |
| Stage 2 | Sauveterre-de-Guyenne | Marmande | 41km | 209m | 68 |
| Stage 3 | Marmande | Buzet-sur-Baïse | 40.4km | 102m | 86 |
| Stage 4 | Buzet-sur-Baïse | Agen | 30.6km | 50m | 100 |
| Excursion 1 | Pont de Thomas | Port-Sainte-Marie and Clermont-Dessous | 20km (round trip) | 91m | 112 |
| Excursion 2 | Écluse l'Auvignon | Nérac | 28.4km (round trip) | 448m | 118 |
| Stage 5 | Agen | Moissac | 45km | 55m | 123 |
| Excursion 3 | Pont Auvillar | Auvillar | 10.5km | 60m | 138 |
| Stage 6 | Moissac | Montauban | 37km | 75m | 142 |
| Stage 7 | Montauban | Toulouse | 43km | 95m | 154 |

*Bordeaux lake is a good place for picnicking (Prologue)*

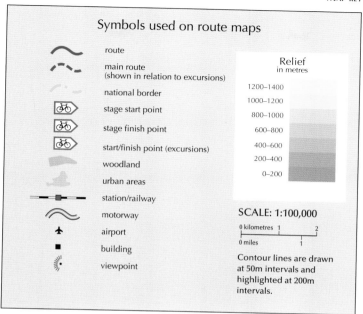

Symbols used on route maps

route

main route
(shown in relation to excursions)

national border

stage start point

stage finish point

start/finish point (excursions)

woodland

urban areas

station/railway

motorway

airport

building

viewpoint

Relief
in metres

1200–1400

1000–1200

800–1000

600–800

400–600

200–400

0–200

SCALE: 1:100,000

0 kilometres  1        2

0 miles               1

Contour lines are drawn
at 50m intervals and
highlighted at 200m
intervals.

## Acknowledgements

Very many thanks to the staff of Voies Navigables de France (VNF) and the people working in local and regional tourist offices for the valuable help and information that they supplied. Special thanks go to my wife Mary and son Oscar for their support and encouragement while I was both cycling and writing. Mary accompanied me on part of the route and her help then was of great value. Thanks too for the help and guidance from the Cicerone team, especially Lesley and Jonathan Williams, Hannah Stevenson and Andrea Grimshaw, and Stephanie Rebello, editor.

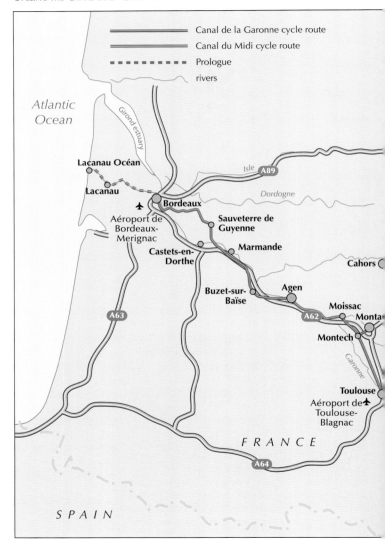

Canal de la Garonne cycle route
Canal du Midi cycle route
Prologue
rivers

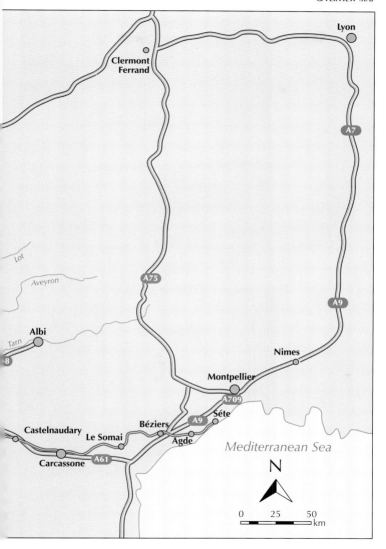

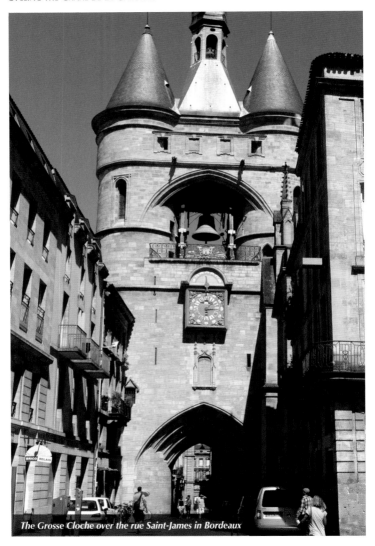

The Grosse Cloche over the rue Saint-James in Bordeaux

# INTRODUCTION

*The Garonne canal is at the heart of this cycle ride*

The Bordeaux region is a cycling paradise of long traffic-free stretches of cycle track with gentle climbs through forests, vineyards, farms and medieval villages. The Garonne canal is at the heart of this. Its 193km asphalted towpath from Castets-en-Dorthe to Toulouse is a dedicated cycle path for most of its length. Occasionally, it uses roads but these are minor with little traffic. Both Bordeaux and Toulouse are cycling cities with a network of tracks that allow you to explore them with ease.

To reach the canal this guide uses another dedicated cycle path to get from Bordeaux to Sauveterre-de-Guyenne; a gentle climb along a converted railway track to this lovely *bastide* town. Minor roads are then followed from Sauveterre-de-Guyenne to the canal.

This guide also includes a prologue from Bordeaux to Lacanau on the Atlantic coast. It follows an old railway line that has been converted to a cycle track which passes through the extensive forests of Les Landes. This allows you to recreate in part a route from the Atlantic to Toulouse. In all, over 490km of cycle routes are described ranging from small detours or longer excursions. They offer you the chance to explore and savour the region to the full. The cycle tracks are specified as departmental roads from which motorised vehicles are excluded meaning that they are maintained to a high standard.

The region between Bordeaux and Toulouse is steeped in history and culture. The soil is fertile and produces an abundance of fruit, vegetables and cereals. Its grasslands feed cattle and sheep. People have populated it since pre-historic times. Its rivers allowed early settlers access the interior; they settled on the riverbanks and eventually villages and towns sprang up.

The area has been invaded and fought over frequently. The Romans were among the first to conquer it and the ruins of their occupation are scattered across the Garonne plain.

Others followed in quick succession each leaving their mark on the architecture and culture of the region.

The original purpose of the Garonne canal was to complete Pierre-Paul Riquet's dream of linking the Atlantic Ocean with the Mediterranean Sea. The idea for some form of canal system had been around since Roman times to obviate the need to circumnavigate the Iberian Peninsula. Riquet instigated the creation of the Canal du Midi from Toulouse to Sète in the 17th century. Prior to this, goods were shipped from Bordeaux to Toulouse by the Garonne river. This was a dangerous stretch of water: there were rapids and shallows – particularly in summer – and floods and high waters in winter. The journey from the sea inland was obviously

## CANAL DE LA GARONNE

The canal runs parallel to the river and thus its original name, Canal latéral à la Garonne. It is also known as the Canal de la Garonne and the Canal de Garonne. You will see signs for the Canal entre deux mers (canal between two seas) which refers to the two canals: Canal de la Garonne joining Bordeaux to Toulouse and the Canal du Midi from Toulouse to Sète. For simplicity, this book uses the English translation, Garonne canal, for the canal from Bordeaux to Toulouse.

Canals need a constant and steady supply of water to work effectively, and the Garonne river provides this for the Garonne canal. The Brienne canal brings river water to the Port Embouchure in Toulouse where it feeds the Garonne canal. The Canal du Midi also opens into this port and so some water from its source, the reservoir in St-Férréol, contributes to the Garonne canal. The water supply is augmented through the subterranean Laboulbène channel in Agen.

against the flow which made it arduous. Heavy rains often made the journey downstream difficult and sometimes treacherous. The Garonne canal overcame these problems and ensured a reliable passage for goods between the two seas.

The Garonne river is always close to the canal. The canal passes close to villages and towns built on the river's banks. The Tarn, Baïse and Lot are major tributaries of the Garonne and you will come close to or cross these on the route. Near Moissac it borders the River Tarn. The canal extension from Montech to Montauban also links to the Tarn.

## REGIONS OF THE CANAL

The route passes through two of France's administrative regions: Nouvelle Aquitaine with Bordeaux as its capital or prefecture and Occitanie whose administrative capital/prefecture is Toulouse. These administrative regions were created in mid-2016 and so you will find maps and signs referring to the previous regions: Aquitaine and Midi-Pyrénées.

The regions are sub-divided into departments. Each French department is numbered alphabetically. They are usually named after a river or rivers running through it. The route passes through: Gironde (33), Lot-et-Garonne (47), Tarn-et-Garonne (82) and Haute-Garonne (31). You will see signs along the route marking the beginning of each department.

## THE CANAL'S CONSTRUCTION

In the 17th century, Louis XIV recognised the commercial and economic security benefits of linking the Atlantic Ocean and the Mediterranean Sea. The journey around the Spanish and Portuguese coast, through the Straits of Gibraltar, was long and perilous. Cargo ships were attacked by pirates, while winter storms sank them. Roads were poor and could not cope with increasing volumes as manufacturing and trade increased. Work began on the Canal du Midi in 1666 and was completed in 1680. It proved to be a great success and continued to operate commercially into the mid-20th century. Despite the difficulty in travelling between Bordeaux and Toulouse, social and economic instability meant that was not until the 19th century that the idea of the canal connection was seriously considered. Jean-Baptiste de Baudre was the bridge and roads engineer chosen to oversee the building of the canal between Toulouse and Castets-en-Dorthe. The project began in 1839, building the canal in stages. The works were completed on 12 March 1856 when the canal's full length was declared navigable.

Despite competition from railways, canal business grew. It was an efficient means of transporting raw materials and agricultural produce such as wood, grain and wine. One advantage it had over the railway was stations were not required to make a stop. As you cycle along you will notice plenty of small harbours or jetties where barges used to stop to load and unload goods.

The canal passed back to state control in 1898. The Voies navigables de France (VNF), the French waterways company, now manages it. Apart from horse, cow and mule-drawn barges, steam-powered boats also plied the waterway. Diesel power took over after World War II. Today's cycle path follows, in the main, the original towpath used by horses. There was commercial traffic on the canal up until the 1970s. It is now used for recreational boating and cruising.

## LOCKS AND BRIDGES

The canal locks are all a standard size and were lengthened and automated in 1973. They are now 40m long allowing them to take a barge of 38.5m. A water slope to avoid the locks near Montech was built in 1974.

The locks are numbered in descending order from 53 at Castets-en-Dorthe to one at Lalande. The numbers are given in brackets in the text. There is a blue sign over the door of each lockkeeper's house giving the name and number of the lock and the distance to the previous and next ones. The locks are often combined with a road bridge and these are referred to as bridge/locks in the text.

Most bridges have a sign giving their name and the distance from Toulouse. It is marked 'PK' which stands for Point Kilométrique (kilometre point). This guide uses some of these as reference points. Some of the modern bridges do not have a sign and there are none near Toulouse.

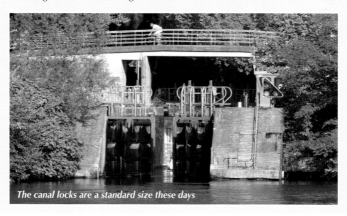

*The canal locks are a standard size these days*

## HISTORY

People have lived in the region between Bordeaux and Toulouse since prehistoric times and traces of their pottery and other artefacts have been found along what was to become the route of the Garonne canal. Artworks created by Cro-Magnon man were discovered in caves at Prignac-et-Marcamps, north of Bordeaux, and archaeological findings suggest that the caves were occupied for almost 60,000 years stretching from 80,000BP (before the present) to 25,000BP. Some evidence points to people of Basque origin being among the early settlers in Aquitaine. They were also the first settlers of Toulouse. It was much later that the Celtic Volcae-Tectosages people spread throughout southwest France in the last six centuries BC and ruled the area around Toulouse. The Celtic Bituriges Viviscila tribe established the port of Burdigala on the banks of the Garonne and this evolved into the present-day Bordeaux.

The Romans entered the region in 121BC to subdue the rebellious Celts along the Mediterranean. Julius Caesar annexed the province following the Gallic Wars 58–60BC. Toulouse, known as Tolosa, was already a flourishing town when the Romans invaded. They relocated the town from the mountains to the plain and built it on a Roman model. It grew in wealth and status and was one of the major cities of the western Empire. A further contribution of the Romans was to promote the development of agriculture and viniculture. After their departure further occupations and conquests followed.

### The Cathar Crusade

The crusade against the Cathars was one of the major historical events in the region. The Cathar belief had

*Roman ruins in Castelculier (Stage 5)*

spread through the region in the 10th century. It was a dualistic form of Christianity which believed that evil came from an evil God and good from a good one. The Cathars prayed and fasted regularly, and the local population in southwest France admired their piety and contrasted it with the lifestyle of the Roman Catholic clerics.

Pierre of Castelnau was a papal legate charged with suppressing the Cathar heresy and the first Inquisitor of Toulouse. In January 1208 Raymond VI met Pierre of Castelnau to persuade him to revoke an excommunication order pronounced against him. The following day, 14 January, some of Raymond's men attacked the legate's party and assassinated Pierre of Castelnau. This murder was the pretext for declaring a crusade against Raymond and his lands were offered as booty. The pope put his legate Arnaud-Amaury in charge.

The crusade brought an army of 50,000 led by Baron de Montfort to the region in June 1209. The conflict was in reality between the nobles of the north and those of the south. It raged across the region for the next five years. Toulouse was besieged unsuccessfully between 26 and 29 June in 1211. Moissac surrendered the following year on 8 September. The southern forces were decisively defeated in the battle of Muret (near Toulouse) in September 1213.

Cathars survived in isolated areas and were ruthlessly pursued by Dominican inquisitors who tortured potential heretics to force them to confess. The persecution stretched as far as Agen where heretics were burnt at the stake in Place de Gravier. The town's last Cathar bishop, Vigoureaux de Barcelone, was burnt in 1236.

## The English in Gascony

'English' is a very loose term when describing those people who ruled both England and Gascony. The Normans conquered England in 1066. Their descendants formed a union with the rulers of Anjou and founded the Plantagenet dynasty that ruled a territory from England to Aquitaine for a period. Anjou formed part of their territory which explains why they are referred to as Angevin kings.

Gascony is also a loose term as the region overlapped with Aquitaine. The Gascon people were Basque in origin and were generally in the south of the region around the river Gironde. Aquitainians were a people living north of the Gironde. The region's borders and the divisions changed up to the French revolution. The terms are used loosely here in line with those used at the time of the events described.

Eleanor of Aquitaine came to power at 15 years of age when her father died in 1137. She married the heir to the French throne, Prince Louis, on 25 July 1137 in Bordeaux's Saint Andre. Prince Louis ascended to the French throne a few weeks later. This brought the two kingdoms together. A disastrous crusade in the holy land exposed rifts between the royal couple and their marriage was finally annulled in 1152 on the grounds of consanguinity.

Two months after her annulment Eleanor married Henry, Duke of Normandy, her third cousin and heir apparent to the English throne. In 1154 he became king of England and Eleanor was then recognised as the queen. The marriage was turbulent and Henry eventually imprisoned his wife for allegedly supporting a rebellion against him. On Henry's death, her son Richard I released her and she oversaw the kingdom while Richard (the Lionheart) was fighting in the crusades. On Richard's death, his brother John took the throne. He proved to be a weak leader and through battle and negotiation lost much of England's kingdom in France – ceding Normandy.

However, the English king's rule did strengthen the trade between the two kingdoms. Toulouse was also under the sway of the English kings as the Count of Toulouse was the English King's vassal. The demand for wine in England contributed to the growth of the region's wine business and the capital generated from wine and other produce formed the King of England's primary income for some time. This led to conflict over Aquitaine with French kings wanting their share of the revenue.

## BASTIDE TOWNS

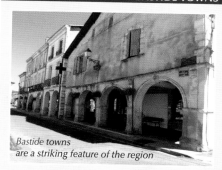

Bastide towns
are a striking feature of the region

*Bastide* towns are a striking feature of the region. There isn't a single agreed definition of what a *bastide* town is, but you recognise them easily when you see them. The name derives from the French word, *bastide*, meaning a provincial house. Generally, *bastides* are defined as any town built at the same time to a clear plan. They normally had a strict grid, often with straight streets. Houses usually had the same or similar designs. They had a marketplace, sometimes covered, at their heart. This was surrounded by *couverts* (arcades). The church was generally close to the square but often set back from it.

Raymond VII of Saint-Gilles, Count of Toulouse, began building *bastides* to replace villages and towns destroyed during the Cathar Crusade. He was permitted to build these under the terms of the Paris Treaty of 1229. This stipulated that these could not be fortified although fortifications were often added later. There were approximately 700 *bastide* towns built between 1222 and 1372 throughout France, with most being in southwest France. There were advantages to living in a *bastide* in medieval times. Towns' people were free men. They had allotments outside the town where they could grow food crops and were also exempt from certain taxes and charges.

Some of the towns are referred to as English *bastides* reflecting the fact that they were built by the French-speaking kings of England from the powerful Angevin Dynasty. Edward I was so impressed by the concept of the *bastide* that he built several in Wales.

There are many examples of *bastides* close to the canal or along the cycle routes covered in this guide. One of the most striking is Montauban on the banks of the Tarn. Its main square, Place Nationale, is built of red brick, two to three storeys high, with double arcades underneath. Créon and Sauveterre-de-Guyenne on the Roger Lapébie cycle track from Bordeaux are good examples of a style that you will see along the length of the route.

## War and turmoil

The Hundred Years' War was in reality a series of skirmishes, battles and occasional invasions rather than constant all-out war. And, of course, it lasted longer than a hundred years as it ran from 1337 to 1453 (116 years). The war was between the Plantagenet and French rulers, among these Edward, Prince of Aquitaine, and known as the Black Prince. Travelling through the region, you will find reference to the dukes, princes and kings involved in the war. Edward's 'Black' title comes from the alleged killing of 3000 people during the siege of Limoges. This was possibly an unfair slur. Inevitably, the long distances

and the cost of the war proved too much for the Plantagenet kings and, in 1475, the Treaty of Picquigny ended the conflict.

The war overlapped with the outbreak of the Black Death which spread across Europe between 1346 and 1353. This was a bacteriological plague spread by fleas carried by rats. Bordeaux was a centre for the spread of the disease as ships from the city spread the plague south to Spain and north to northern France and England.

The region was never far from war. The French Wars of Religion also engulfed it. Sometimes referred to as the Huguenot War this pitched Protestants against Catholics, and the wars threw France into turmoil. Montauban was one of the strongholds of Protestantism and celebrates this tradition to this present.

The country's economic and social state improved during the 19th century. Urbanisation meant that fewer people produced their own food. Improved transport infrastructure through the waterways and railways meant that it was easier to get goods to the new urban markets. Producers began to concentrate on producing specific crops such as wine in the south of France. This concentration may have contributed to the devastating outbreak of phylloxera, a plague of aphids that fed on the vines and destroyed them. These pests were introduced from America where the vines were resistant, but they left the French wine industry devastated for decades.

The French government relocated to Bordeaux for brief periods during the Franco-Prussian war (1870), World War I and II. It moved from Bordeaux to Vichy during the Nazi occupation in World War II. Bordeaux, because of its port, was occupied directly. The border between Vichy France (the part under the subservient French government) and Nazi occupied regions was inland of Bordeaux close to La Réole. Vichy France, as it was known, lasted from 1940 to 1942 when the whole country came under direct Nazi control. Toulouse was a major centre of resistance to Nazi rule.

The daring cockleshell operation is wartime exploit which stands out. It involved an attack by British

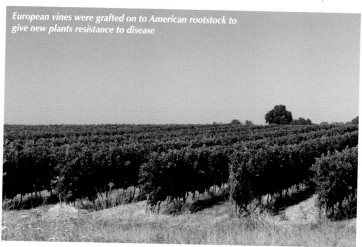

European vines were grafted on to American rootstock to give new plants resistance to disease

commandos on ships moored in Bordeaux harbour. Ten British marines were carried to the outer reaches of the Gironde estuary in a submarine, HMS *Tuna*, in December 1942. They were launched in collapsible canoes, known as cockleshells, to paddle 120km up the estuary to Bordeaux harbour and place explosive charges on ships breaking the Allies embargo. Paddy Ashdown's excellent account of this operation, *A Brilliant Little Operation: The Cockleshell Heroes and the Most Courageous Raid of World War II* is a great read to accompany your cycle. Paddy Ashdown's other book about the region, *Game of Spies: The Secret Agent, the Traitor and the Nazi, Bordeaux 1942–1944*, captures the heroism and treachery that marked the French resistance's actions during the Nazi occupation. Again, it is an excellent companion while cycling in the region.

Allen Massie's four Bordeaux-based detective novels, which describe the work of his hero, Superintendent Lannes, give a strong sense of what life must have been like living under the Nazis.

The end of World War II brought recovery and development. Toulouse for example became a major centre for the aeronautic industry. It is now an internationally important technological hub. Bordeaux's recovery was somewhat slower. It only really began to throw off its dowdy image in the 1990s. Its centre and docklands have been redeveloped to make it the jewel that it now is.

## CULTURE

The mix of rule by English kings and non-conformist Toulouse nobility fostered an artistic temperament and a *joie de vivre*. That spirit continues today and each town or village has its own celebrations or festivals. Open-air concerts are common in the summer while communal parties are scattered throughout the spring, summer and autumn.

Toulouse offers a range of festivals from its international arts festival in May and June with exhibits in historic buildings along the Garonne to its summer festival (Toulouse d'Été) in July and August. Flamenco dancing, piano music, techno, electronica and jazz all feature at some point. Music and the arts are constantly present on the streets and in bars, cafés and music venues across the city.

Festival Off is a free part of Montauban's Montauban en Scènes Festival which celebrates music, dance and performance. The festival itself draws nationally famous performers and large crowds.

Agen offers a more unusual festival, the Big Prune Show, a three-day celebration of the prune with concerts, markets, tastings and street performances. It takes place in late August or early September and coincides with the start of the school year.

Bordeaux has several major wine festivals and its international arts festival takes place in October. Food and wine festivals are scattered through the summer and autumn months. The Climax Festival is in mid-September and has a rock focus.

The major towns and cities offer opera, concerts, drama and ballet throughout the year but especially from late autumn to spring. The local tourist offices will advise you on what's on, when and where.

You will also see plenty of sporting activities as you move through the region – including cycle races. Boules, a form of bowling, is common along the canal and other routes. These range from casual games between friends to competitions with hundreds taking part for large stakes under floodlights. This is also rugby country and cities and towns along the route are home to major teams: Toulouse, Agen, Montauban and Bordeaux Bègles.

## WILDLIFE

The canal and surrounding countryside support abundant wildlife and you will see this as you cycle. Wildflowers grow along the verges of cycle tracks. The canal and rivers teem with fish and invertebrates. Giant dragonflies dance in front of you, while kingfishers and other birds flash overhead. Herons stand motionless at the canal's edges waiting for a fish, lizard, snake or frog to betray their position. Bats fill the evening sky.

*A heron beside the canal near the Poule à Velo (Stage 5)*

Coypu are now a common sight along the canal

The area covered in the prologue, 'From Bordeaux to the Atlantic', provides a greater opportunity to observe larger mammals such as deer and wild boar; smaller mammals such as rabbits and hares are regular sights. You are very likely to see a coypu swimming in the canal or grazing on its banks. These are the descendants of animals that escaped from fur farms and established themselves along the waterway's length.

## CYCLING THE GARONNE CANAL

It is important to divide the route up to suit your own capability and interest. There are plenty of places along the way worth visiting. This guide divides the route into seven stages with an additional long prologue and a very short epilogue – these divisions may not suit everyone and there are plenty of interim stopping places indicated. The stages are:

- Bordeaux to Sauveterre-de-Guyenne
- Sauveterre-de-Guyenne to Marmande
- Marmande to Buzet-sur-Bäise
- Buzet-sur-Bäise to Agen
- Agen to Moissac
- Moissac to Montauban
- Montauban to Toulouse.

In addition, the guide includes detours to sights close to the canal and longer excursions into the surrounding countryside. The prologue goes from Bordeaux to the Atlantic coast at Lacanau, a holiday seaside resort, which is a return trip of 135km. The route from Bordeaux through Sauveterre-de-Guyenne joins the canal at Fontet village 10km after its beginning. The guide includes a description of the route from there to the start of the canal at Castets-en-Dorthe and back – a round trip of 20km. It includes the canal extension to Montauban which some cyclists pressed for time may wish to skip. Other excursions are to:

- Porte-Sainte-Marie and Clermont-Dessous (Excursion 1)
- Nérac (Excursion 2)
- Auvillar (Excursion 3)

There are over 490km of cycling described in this guide including all detours, excursions and return trips. Those who want a shorter cycle may concentrate on the trip from Bordeaux to Toulouse and leave out any side or return trips. This is 281km in total. The canal is 193km long. Those planning a longer cycle should consider some or all of the additional trips. Reasonably fit cyclists should be able to complete all of the routes in two weeks. Those travelling the canal by boat, or living or holidaying in the region, will be able to use the guide to plan day or overnight trips.

Those looking for short one-day cycles can make return trips along the canal or take trains to one station and cycle to another. Some of the best stations for this are: La Réole, Marmande, Tonneins and Agen on the Bordeaux side and Montauban,

*The circular grain market in Place de la Halle, Auvillar (Excursion 3)*

Grisolles, Castelnau-d'Estrétefonds and Saint-Jory on the Toulouse side.

## WHEN TO GO

You can cycle these routes all year and many locals do. The weather in winter can be wet and cold with storms blowing from the Atlantic. The average rainfall is 100mm in December rising to 110mm in January with rain falling on average every second day. Temperatures average between 6°C and 7°C with a daily average of three or four hours of sunshine in these months.

In contrast, the months from May to August have average temperatures of between 23°C and 26°C. May does, however, have a relatively high average rainfall – up to 100mm. Spring comes relatively early and the routes are usually pleasant to cycle from mid-April onwards. The lengthening days in May see the return of swallows and other migrants. Farmers are active in the fields and the early crops are beginning to ripen.

Summer is hot with long days and warm nights. The sunflowers bloom in the fields beside the path and fruits ripen in the orchards close by. The heat brings out the midges and mosquitoes which can be irritating especially given the close proximity of water. There are plenty of festivals and village fêtes during these months. The path is lined with wildflowers with a myriad of butterflies flitting from one to another. Bear in mind that the region does get crowded in July and August and accommodation can be difficult to find, especially at bank holidays and festival weekends. Campsites get crowded too. The final holiday weekend in August can be particularly difficult and you need to book in advance.

The summer warmth seeps into the autumn. The orchards' fruits are ripe and the grapes are harvested and towns and villages celebrate the harvest. Autumn, like spring, is an ideal season for cycling with warm but not stiflingly hot weather. Accommodation is also easier to find during spring and autumn and prices are generally lower. Be aware, however, that some campsites may not be open and there are fewer markets, festivals and outdoor events.

## GETTING THERE

**By air**
The Garonne canal is easily reached as it begins and ends in two of France's main cities. Both cities have major airports with good international connections. Blagnac airport in Toulouse has flights from London Stansted, Heathrow and Luton, Birmingham, Bristol and Manchester; from Dublin and Shannon in Ireland as well as from within France and from most European countries together with Tunisia and Algeria in North Africa.

Merignac Airport in Bordeaux has flights from London Stansted,

Luton and Gatwick, Edinburgh, Glasgow, Birmingham, Bristol and Southampton; from Belfast, Dublin and Cork in Ireland and from similar destinations to those serving Toulouse.

Low-cost carriers such as easyJet, Flybe and Ryanair serve these airports. The best way to find out who is flying to either airport and from where is by consulting the airport websites: www.bordeaux.aeroport.fr and www.toulouse.aeroport.fr.

You should advise your airline when you book your flight if you plan to bring a bike. Airlines limit the number of bikes that they carry on each flight. You will be required to turn pedals inwards or take them off entirely, and must also fix the handlebars sideways. You must pack the bike in a hard or soft holder, deflating the tyres to avoid them bursting under decompression. Airline charges for carrying bikes vary; expect to pay approximately €50 per flight. Airlines do not normally carry electric bikes.

**By car**
Bordeaux and Toulouse are easily reached by road. Bordeaux is between six and eight hours' drive from channel ports. The French motorway network will deliver you to the canal from any of France's borders in 12 hours. The motorways are tolled and expensive for a long journey, for example the tolls from Calais to Bordeaux are €158.63. You can calculate your route and the total toll charges using the French motorway

companies' website: www.autoroutes.fr.

The A10 motorway links Bordeaux with northern France. The A62 goes between Bordeaux and Toulouse and is close to the canal along its length. The A61 approaches Toulouse from the south.

It is possible to park along the length of the canal. The canal ports have limited parking available, most of which is free. You can also park in the villages and small towns on the canal and this is often free. There are car parks in the two cities which permit long-term and more secure parking. Some of these offer a special weekly rate. Hotels and guesthouses may allow you to park your car for a few days, even after your stay, but you should arrange this in advance.

**By train**
Bordeaux and Toulouse are major rail centres. The train line between the two cities runs beside the canal for much of its length. The stations close to the canal are La Reole, Marmande, Tonneins, Aiguillon Lot et Garonne, Port Ste Marie, Agen, La Magistere, Valence d'Agen, Moissac, Castelsarrasin, Montauban Ville Bourbon, Montbartier, Dieupentale, Grisolles, Castelnau d'Estretefonds, Saint-Jory, Lacourtensourt and Toulouse Matabiau. SNCF (Société Nationale Chemins de Fer), the train company, operates buses to other towns along the canal. These do not carry bicycles.

The railway company's website (www.sncf.com) gives information on which trains carry bicycles and whether there is a charge for these. TGVs, the French rapid rail system, does carry bikes but these need to be packed in bags. Occasionally, they take bikes unbagged in dedicated spaces. Some fellow cyclists have booked bikes onto TGVs only to be told, at the station, that bikes were not accepted.

Intercités and TER (Transport Express Régional) accept bikes. Intercités charge for them and you must book in advance. There is only space for a limited number on each train so book as far in advance as possible. TERs generally accept bikes without a charge or pre-booking. Check in advance as the regulations can change from train to train. It is best to travel mid-morning, mid-afternoon or later in the evening. SNCF uses a bike symbol to indicate trains that accept bikes.

Bikes are stored in different ways on trains. In some, you can wheel your bike on board and lean it against upturned seats. In others, you hang them from hooks provided. Make sure you remove anything that might fall off during the journey.

The Sunday evening trains on the Bordeaux–Toulouse line can be very crowded and unpleasant. July and August are the worst months for travelling with a bike but weekends and public holidays can be busy throughout the year.

Bike trailers are forbidden on French trains. Railway staff are not permitted to help you lift your bike off or on the train – they are not being difficult or obstructive when they do not help. Cyclists usually help each other. Tandem bikes may also be refused. Bear in mind that you may have to change platforms when travelling and you should allow time for this when booking as you may have to carry your bike up and down flights of stairs.

Eurostar offers a registered baggage service, EuroDespatch, operating between London, Paris and Lille Eurostar terminals. They guarantee the bike will be available for collection within 24 hours of registration and advise you to send your bike ahead so that it is there when you arrive. Eurostar charge £30 for this service. Check Eurostar's website (www.eurostar.com) if you plan to travel with them. Within France, SNCF provide a similar door-to-door service (home or train station) with an €80 charge. Enquire about this at a train station or find further details at www.sncf.com/en/services/luggage.

**Passports and travel requirements**
Travellers from the UK and Ireland must have a valid passport or passport card to travel in France. This may change when the UK leaves the EU. Your passport must be in date for the length of your stay in France. France accepts identity cards from EU citizens. As the UK and Ireland do not operate all of the Schengen agreement

(which allows free travel without border controls between participating countries) a residency or visa for another EU country does not give you an automatic right to enter France. The French embassy website (UK), www.ambafrance-uk.org, gives information on visa requirements.

Australian, Canadian, New Zealand and US citizens do not need a visa for a stay of less than 90 days but require a full passport. Non-EU visitors to France must have, ready for presentation at the border, documentary evidence of the reason for their visit, means of support for its duration and details of their accommodation arrangements.

## ACCOMMODATION

There is a wide range of places to stay on the various routes, ranging from expensive to very basic. There are hotels, hostels, chambres d'hôtes (bed and breakfast), gîtes (holiday homes for rent), camping and chalets in campsites. Airbnb offers a range of properties but mainly in the larger centres. It is worth checking as there are some in smaller or more rural places. See Appendix B for a comprehensive list of accommodation options on or near the route, along with contact details.

The hotels vary from chains to small boutique ones. Chain hotels in larger towns are usually cheaper. You pay extra for breakfast in most. Chain hotels such as B&B and Ibis are situated close to the canal in Toulouse. The rooms are usually but not always en suite. You will find Mercure and Novotel chain hotels in Bordeaux centre.

The Intercontinental Grand Hotel in Bordeaux may charge up to €500 a night for a room in high season. Other

*Chambres d'hôtes provide an opportunity to stay in French homes*

five-star hotels charge over €150 per room per night; chains charge between €50 and €100; smaller hotels may charge less than €60 a room. There is generally a supplement for an additional person.

The quality of smaller French hotels varies widely and you should check the room before you accept it. Cheaper hotels may have very limited facilities, and not all rooms are the same. You may find that the bathroom and toilet are shared by everyone on the corridor. Most rooms have a hand basin, while it is possible that you may be offered a room with a shower but no toilet.

Chambres d'hôtes are the French equivalent of British bed and break-fast. As with small hotels, they vary in price and quality. Usually, the quality is good with some being excellent, but do check the rooms in advance. Most chambres d'hôtes offer evening meals and these are usually eaten commu-nally. The standard of catering is gen-erally very good and most use local produce. Prices vary greatly, with some charging over €100 per room per night but most charging between €40 and €90 for bed and breakfast, with an evening meal costing an extra €15 to €20. Supplements for a second person apply. Some hotels and cham-bres d'hôtes offer a special deal for dinner, bed and breakfast known as soirée étape, which is excellent value.

Gîtes are self-catering and may be a holiday home, wood chalet or an apartment. They are usually booked in advance and for at least a week with changeovers on Saturday morning. On occasions you may be able to hire one for an overnight or a few nights' stay. You are generally expected to provide your own towels and sheets although some owners will provide these for cyclists. Gîtes are usually well equipped and you are expected to clean and tidy fully before you leave.

Camping is a great option and there are campsites close to all of the routes described in this guide. The sites range from basic – often municipal – to five-star with swim-ming pools, restaurants and tennis courts. Larger campsites may be noisy during the high season and most are closed between October and April. Pitches for tents cost between €12 and €30 a night. Some campsites rent chalets by the night if they are avail-able; these are normally rented by the week though. There are extra charges for more people, dogs, electricity and vehicles.

All prices increase during the high season.

## FOOD AND DRINK

The region is the centre for some of the best food and drink in France. You move from the rich Atlantic foods in the Gironde to the Mediterranean influenced foods in Toulouse. It is a premier wine-producing region and Bordeaux is known as the top wine-producing area in the world.

Chefs pride themselves on using local produce to create their dishes. Bordeaux cuisine is heavily meat-based. 'A la Bordelaise' means cooking a dish in the Bordeaux style. This is a sauce made with bone marrow, shallots and red, or sometimes white, wine. This is used with meat, fish and eggs or shellfish so vegetarians or pescatarians should avoid this sauce. Suckling lamb (Agneau de Pauillac) and oysters from the Arcachon basin (Huîtres d'Arcachon) are two of the regions famed dishes. Toulouse has its own sausage made with smoked bacon, red wine and garlic. A regional delicacy served in Toulouse is *cassoulet*. This is a bean and meat stew which originated in nearby Castelnaudary. Another stew which is less well known but typical of the region is *garbure* which is a winter dish based on pork and beans.

You see fruit and vegetables growing beside the route as you cycle. Vegetables come into season earlier than in northern Europe and so you can enjoy these at the start of the summer. Fruit production is a major regional industry and you will see apples, plums, peaches, kiwis and figs growing near the path. Fish in the region is excellent and comes from both seas: the Atlantic and the Mediterranean.

## Restaurants and cafés

The region boasts very many top-quality restaurants such as le Chapon Fin in Bordeaux, Mariottat in Agen and

*There are plenty of good-value bistros, restaurants and cafés along the route*

Michel Sarran in Toulouse. There are plenty of good-value restaurants, bistros and cafés along the route. Some are only open for the tourist season while others are open all year round. The latter tend to offer better value and quality.

Set meals are the cheapest option and lunches are the best value. You will find set lunches costing as little as €12 per person but usually a bit more and this will include the set starter, main course and sometimes a dessert. The price may also include a quarter-litre (*un quart*) of the house wine.

Vegetarians are rarely able to benefit from set meals as the main course is usually fish or meat. The term vegetarian is often defined

29

loosely in France and waiters may try to serve fish or chicken as vegetarian options. Some stuffed vegetables may contain meat. Salads are ubiquitous and usually very good. Goat's cheese and beetroot is normally delicious.

Traditional restaurants generally observe strict opening times although there are some exceptions often near railway stations. Restaurants generally stop taking orders for lunch at 2.30pm and orders for dinner are not usually accepted after 9.30pm.

### Shops and markets
Picnics are one of the more enjoyable aspects of cycling along the canal or in the countryside generally. *Boulangeries* (bakeries) and *pâtisseries*

*Local markets offer fresh, locally produced foods*

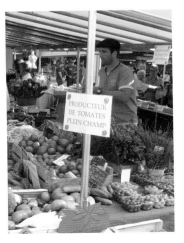

(pastry shops) are at the heart of French towns and villages. Baguettes are excellent for picnics and great value but only stay fresh for a few hours.

Shopping is easy along the route. The choice is extensive ranging from hypermarkets and supermarkets to small local stores or producers selling from their premises. In addition, there are markets, at least weekly, in most towns and villages.

Smaller shops generally open early in the morning at 7.30am and close between 12.30pm and 3.30pm in the afternoon. They close in the evening around 7pm. Some may open on Sunday morning.

Markets are full of life and colour. You can buy practically everything from fruit and vegetables to clothes and hardware. The markets usually begin at 8am and finish at 12pm. There are some evening and night markets in summer, often as part of festivals. Markets are held in the main square or along the main street. The two cities, Bordeaux and Toulouse, have markets on most days.

## YOUR BIKE

### Buying or renting a bike
Taking your bike on a plane can be difficult and expensive. An alternative is to buy or rent in France. Second-hand bikes are relatively cheap in the major cities and towns, but may be in short supply in the high season.

## CYCLING HOLIDAY COMPANIES

To avoid having to organise your own bike and carry your own luggage, another option is to use a specialist company offering cycling holidays. These outfits can arrange basic bike hire and accommodation through to transporting baggage, providing lunches and guiding groups of cyclists. These companies can cater for individuals and groups. Large travel agents offer this service through local providers although you can contact providers directly if you want a more tailored response.

Bikes are good value in France and buying one new is another option. Major sports stores such as Decathlon (www.decathlon.fr) and Intersport (www.intersport.fr) sell bikes at reasonable prices. There are specialist bike shops along the route carrying a good range of models. Large supermarkets also stock bikes, especially in summer.

E-bikes have become popular and the route is perfectly suited to them. Firms offer them for long- or short-term hire in Bordeaux or Toulouse as well as in some of the major towns.

There are plenty of companies offering standard bikes for hire, although if you plan to use it for more than a few days then buying

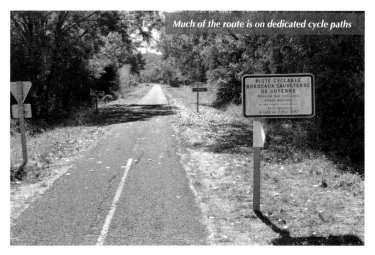
*Much of the route is on dedicated cycle paths*

a second-hand bike may be a better option. Daily rental is usually around €15. You should hire bikes from companies who have their own mechanics and workshops, as hired bikes deteriorate during the season.

Note: having hired or bought a bike, check which brake lever operates which brake before you start to cycle!

**Type of bike**
You can cycle the route using any type of standard bike. The entire path is asphalted excluding a few cobble-stoned sections usually on aqueducts. You can use narrow tyred racing-style bikes which are fast but may not be the best for carrying large, heavy bags. Standard touring and all-terrain-bikes (ATBs) will have no difficulties coping with the terrain.

Good brakes are essential. Consider using quick-release wheels as you should assume that you will suffer at least one puncture. A gel-filled saddle or saddle cover give additional comfort and will absorb harder knocks. A suspension saddle serves the same purpose.

Fit a waterbottle holder to your bike frame. These are easily attached to most bikes. Ensure that your bottle fits snugly into the holder.

You will need a rear carrier if you use panniers. This should be strong enough to take the weight of your bags and a tent if you plan to camp. Most carriers support a maximum load of 20kg.

Fit front, rear and spoke reflectors. Bring and wear a high-visibility jacket in low light. You must have front and rear lights in the hours of darkness; detachable ones are best to avoid theft. However, lights will be insufficient for cycling on unlit paths – especially the prologue to the Atlantic.

**Taking care of your bike**
You should have your bike serviced before you start your journey. Carry a repair kit including:

* puncture repair kit
* spanners and Allen keys to fit all nuts and bolts
* pump (mini foot pump preferably)
* spoke tightener
* screwdriver matching the screws on your bike
* two replacement tubes
* replacement tyre (folded up)
* replacement spokes and screws.
* spare brake pads, especially if you have disc brakes, as they are not always stocked

Learn how to change a tube and tyre before you leave. Get your local bike shop to show you how to adjust your brakes and gears. Find out which nuts you need to tighten regularly, for example, you should check the nuts on your carrier daily as these can work loose and shear.

You should make sure that your tyres are fully inflated each day as this helps protect against punctures. There are bike shops in the main centres and along the route; these will repair bikes and sell the supplies that you may need (a list of bike repair shops is given in Appendix C).

## WHAT TO TAKE

There is a golden rule for packing for a cycle trip: lay out everything you want to take and leave half behind.

The season determines what clothes you should take. The late autumn and early spring may be cold particularly at night. Thermal underclothes and socks are lightweight and extremely useful. Cycling gloves, a warm cycling jacket and long cycling trousers will also protect against the cold. Lightweight, breathable waterproof tops and leggings are useful all

year round for poor weather in any season.

You should bring light, cool clothes in summer. Light cycling tops and shorts are essential; these should be easy to wash and dry.

Shorts should cover your thighs even on the upstroke when pedalling to avoid the risk of sunburn. Cycling shorts with a chamois leather pad are very useful; wash them daily to avoid saddle sores. You should also consider bringing a tub of Sudocrem to help prevent saddle sores and/or treat them. This is not generally available in France.

Sunglasses are useful throughout the year but essential in summer. Buy pairs with removable lenses and replace the darkened glass with low

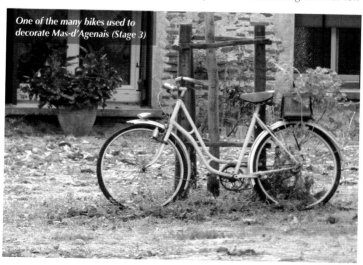

*One of the many bikes used to decorate Mas-d'Agenais (Stage 3)*

light lenses in the evening as a protection against insects and dust.

A list of items includes:

- sunhat and sunglasses
- sun cream
- anti-mosquito cream
- lotion for treating bites
- small first aid kit with bandages, scissors, tweezers (for thorns or splinters), antiseptic cream and Sudocrem
- any medication you take regularly
- spare prescription glasses or contact lenses.

**Your luggage**
A handlebar bag is very useful for holding valuables such as a camera and mobile phone, etc. Bags with a clear plastic map holder on top are particularly handy.

Use panniers to carry your personal effects; avoid taking a heavy rucksack if you plan to cycle for several days as it can chafe your shoulders and back. Panniers are available in a range of shapes and sizes. You can buy high-quality back panniers that are waterproof and easy to secure. Saddlebag-style panniers (three bags joined together) are another alternative; one sits on the pannier and the other two on either side.

Make sure that the bags do not impede your pedalling. Use panniers you can adjust to allow your feet free movement. Some cyclists use plastic covers to protect their luggage from dust.

Those wanting to carry a lot of gear should consider a bike trailer. These hold more but are harder to manoeuvre. The paths are wide enough for both two-wheeled or single-wheeled ones.

## HEALTH AND SAFETY

**Medical services**
France's health service is very good. Most medium-sized villages have a medical centre combining medical and paramedical services. Pharmacies (look for flashing green crosses) dispense medicines and pharmacists give advice on basic illnesses or injuries.

Visitors from the EU and EEA countries should carry an in-date European Health Insurance Card (EHIC) from their own health service. This card covers any medical treatment resulting from accident or injury. You may apply for an EHIC via the UK government's website (www.gov.uk/european-health-insurance-card).

General practices usually display their opening hours on the clinic's door or wall together with a number for an out-of-hours service. French doctors still make home visits and may come to see you if you are too unwell to reach the surgery. Doctors and pharmacies are paid at the time of visiting but hospitals will bill your home address for treatment received in France not covered under the EHIC scheme.

Contact the Service d'Aide Medicale Urgence (SAMU) in the event of a life-threatening illness or accident; their telephone number is 15. They may connect you to an English-speaking specialist or pass your call to a private ambulance service. You can also use the general emergency number 112.

## Insurance

All cyclists are advised to take out proper health and travel insurance. It is essential for those without the protection of the EHIC and advisable for those entitled to it. This should cover unlikely eventualities such as repatriation in the event of serious illness or accident, prolonged hospitalisation and the cost of major medical procedures.

## Preparation

You can cycle the route at your own pace, but cycling can be a vigorous activity and you should have a full physical check-up if you have not cycled or taken exercise for a long time.

It is best to cycle at home before your trip to the south of France. A small amount of training will help to avoid stiffness, aches and pulled muscles or tendons. The key is to build up gradually from short cycles – under half an hour – to longer, half-day rides. Remember – cycle on the right in France.

## Helmets and clothing

The most important precaution you should take when cycling is to wear a helmet, as it will greatly reduce the

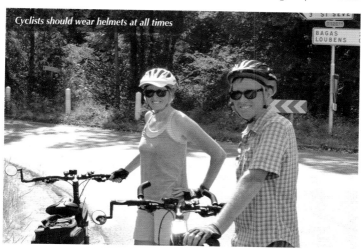

Cyclists should wear helmets at all times

risk of serious head injury. A fall is a constant potential hazard. There is a temptation to discard your helmet in hot weather but do not. Pour water on your head or stick it under the tap. French law requires children under 12 years of age to wear a helmet when cycling or travelling as a passenger on a bicycle.

Wear brightly coloured jerseys. You cross roads regularly and you cycle on them at several points and you need to be visible to motorists. The French countryside is sparsely populated and thus poorly lit. Use front and rear lights from dusk onwards; if possible avoid cycling at night but if you must wear a hi-vis vest or jacket.

## Weather extremes

The south of France gets very hot in summer particularly as you move from the coast towards Toulouse. Inland, it can top 40°C during the day, and on some nights the temperature remains over 30°C. The Bordeaux region is cooler than Toulouse with pleasant daytime temperatures, although it can become very hot at the peak of the summer.

Always carry water and drink copious amounts; a good rule of thumb is one litre per hour. Drink before you feel thirsty and supplement your salt intake if you perspire a lot.

Sunburn is another potential risk for cyclists. It only takes 30 minutes of direct sunshine to burn and this can ruin the rest of the cycle ride. Use lots of high-factor suntan lotion, putting it on all exposed skin, and keep a cycling jersey on at all times.

The canal crosses the Garonne plain and there is a risk of flooding in very wet weather. Summer thunderstorms as well as winter rains can cause flash flooding. Villages along the canal have sirens which sound when there is a flood risk. You should take advice if you hear the sirens and move uphill from the canal or river immediately.

## Bites, stings and other hazards

There is standing water close to the path and this creates ideal conditions for mosquitoes and midges. Mosquitoes are more active in the evening and at night. Wear long sleeves and long-legged bottoms, paying special attention to wrists, ankles, neck and head. Creams or sprays containing DEET give good protection to adult skin.

You will also meet wasps, hornets and bees in all seasons but winter. You can treat stings with over-the-counter creams or lotions. Watch out for an allergic reaction and seek immediate treatment. You should attend a doctor if stung in or near the mouth or eyes.

Rats live beside and swim in the canal. Canal water may therefore harbour Weil's or other diseases. The canal receives run-off and effluent from farms and the water is undrinkable. Never swim in the canal, even

## EMERGENCY NUMBERS

Use the following numbers in the event of an emergency:

- Medical/SAMU 15
- Police/Gendarmerie 17
- Fire/Pompier 18
- European emergency number 112

The pan-European number 112 works in any EU country from any phone. Use this if you are using a mobile.

though you may see local children doing so; it is forbidden and may put your health at risk. Wash thoroughly should you get wet with canal water.

The canal locks are potentially dangerous as they are deep and you risk being held underneath the water should you fall in. Treat the locks with respect.

Walkers and other cyclists are the greatest hazards to cyclists. People engrossed in their mobile phones are often unaware of their surroundings and pose a risk to others on the path. Give phone users a wide berth.

## SECURITY

The canal and cycle paths are generally safe both in terms of personal safety and for your bike and goods. The people of the region are friendly and courteous and police patrol towns and villages regularly. That said, you should take normal precautions against crime.

Lock your bike any time you leave it unattended. Make sure that you carry your valuables with you and hidden; carry money, passport and credit cards separately. Keep cameras and other valuables in a bag that you can detach easily and carry with you.

Insure yourself against theft and loss of, or damage to, your belongings, and check if your policy covers theft of your bicycle. Should you have the misfortune to lose your valuables, or be robbed, report this to the police and get a receipt. Insurance policies require this. They also require that you keep your goods or money safely; goods left unattended or unsecured are not covered.

## MAPS

The Institut Géographique National (IGN) produces maps covering the route and excursions. Use 1:100,000 maps in the TOP 100 series. Maps numbered TOP 100145, TOP100160, TOP100161 and TOP100168 cover the route from the Atlantic to Toulouse. These are available from local shops and https://ignrando.fr.

Canal entre deux mers signage

## MONEY AND COMMUNICATIONS

France's currency is the euro. You can withdraw money from ATM machines found in most towns and villages. Contactless payment is becoming commonplace. Larger bank branches and hotels may exchange dollars, sterling and other widely used currencies. Smaller bank branches have stopped changing foreign currencies and will not change larger denomination euro notes such as the €500 bill.

European bill-pay mobiles should work in France and roaming charges for calls and texts should match home charges for phones from the EU. Data charges may vary. Check with your provider if you are from outside the EU or using a pay-as-you-go phone. Internet cafés offer internet telephone services too. There are still a few public phones in some villages and towns; you can buy a card for these in a *tabac* (newsagent) if you want to use them.

Wi-Fi (pronounced 'wee-fee' in French) is generally available in cafés, bars and hotels. Some hotels may charge for their premium services. There is also free Wi-Fi available in certain public areas in Bordeaux and Toulouse. Some tourist offices provide a free service, but these are often limited.

## USING THIS GUIDE

For each stage there is a box giving route information such as the start point, length of the stage, accumulated climb, type of terrain encountered, IGN map number and optional detours. The canal rises from 33m above sea level in Castets-en-Dorthe to 136m in Toulouse so that the accumulated climb on any stage along the canal is relatively small.

There is a brief overview of the day's ride at the start. Stage maps are provided at a scale of 1:100,000, except where stated otherwise. The excursions have route information including the start point, the total distance for the round trip, the terrain and relevant IGN map. All places on the maps are shown in **bold** in the text. For each city, town or village passed an indication is given of the facilities available (accommodation, refreshments, camping, tourist office, cycle shop, station) when the guide was written. Appendix A gives

the distances between locks on the canal and the accumulated distance from the start; Appendix B gives a comprehensive (but not exhaustive) list of accommodation options on or near the route along with contact details; Appendix C gives information that may be of use on the route, such as contact details for tourist information centres and bike repair shops; Appendix D is a glossary of useful French terms which you may wish to arm yourself with for your journey; and Appendix E recommends some further reading about the region.

### Which bank?

We refer to riverbanks as being 'left' or 'right' depending on whether they are on the left or right of the direction in which the river flows. Canal water should flow as little as possible.

*The canal in summer*

39

Technically, the canal water flows from Toulouse (136m above sea level) to Castets-en-Dorthe (33m above). This guide uses the term 'northern' bank to refer to the 'right' and 'southern' to the 'left' bank for clarity – usually both terms are included for certainty. The towpath on the Montech to Montauban canal is on the east bank, only. The route does at times change banks, and these changes are highlighted in sidebar text in this guide. Be sure to follow instructions, even where the path appears to continue on the other side.

## FRENCH TERMS

There are certain French words and phrases which you will come across frequently cycling the canal path. This guide also uses them frequently.

- **appellation d'origine controlée (AOC)** – a French government run programme that certifies a product's regional origin
- **cave** – literally a cellar but also used for a building where wine is produced and/or sold
- **chambre/maison d'hôte** – bed and breakfast
- **chateau** – castle, large house or imposing building
- **écluse** – canal lock
- **halte nautique** – harbour or mooring place for boats
- **moulin** – mill
- **passerelle** – bridge for either pedestrians or cyclists
- **point relais** – meeting place or intermediate point on the route
- **pont** – bridge
- **voie vert** – cycle track (literally greenway)

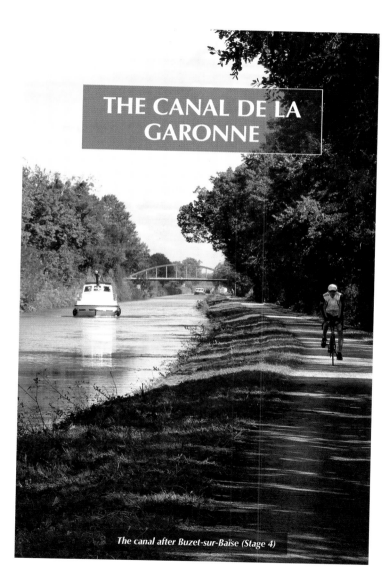

# THE CANAL DE LA GARONNE

*The canal after Buzet-sur-Baïse (Stage 4)*

## BORDEAUX

Bordeaux bustles. From the crescent-shaped riverfront, giving it the alternative name 'Port of the Moon', to the cathedral of Saint-André the city teems with life. Approximately half of the city is classified as a UNESCO heritage site. Its magnificent classical and neo-classical buildings lead you from the waterfront into its heart. The pedestrianised streets, cafés, shops and restaurants buzz. University students add an extra exuberance.

The city is the starting point for the prologue and the first stage of this cycle, but it is well worth exploring in its own right. A short route described below (see Cycling the quays) gives great views of the city and the Gironde estuary, formed by the meeting of the Garonne and Dordogne rivers upstream from the city.

The city straddles the Gironde. It was the centre of the wine trade and its buildings reflect the wealth that it generated. Wine was only one commodity traded. Bordeaux was a major port for trade with French colonies importing and re-exporting coffee, peanuts and cocoa and, more sinisterly, slaves.

The city is easy to explore by bike, public transport or on foot. There is a well-developed cycle lane network, and its comprehensive tram and bus system serves the city and suburbs. The city's main attractions are all within walking distance with a few exceptions and these are easy to reach by bike.

Bordeaux's history reflects that of the surrounding countryside. Settled since before Roman times, it has been colonised by Romans, Visigoths, Normans, English, Saracens and Nazis. It has been the region's capital since Roman times and it has benefitted from the regional successes and suffered when its hinterland was laid waste by war or disease.

*Place de la Bourse*

The Place de la Bourse (Stock Exchange Place, or literally Wallet Place) is one of Bordeaux's striking attractions. It was built as a royal square in honour of King Louis XV between 1730 and 1755. The stock market was on the northern side while the National Customs Museum is on the south of the square.

Le Miroir d'Eau is the largest urban water mirror and is between the Place de la Bourse and the river. The 2cm of water reflect the square's buildings and it is a favourite summer play area for adults and children.

The city's gates are worth viewing. Port Cailhau celebrates King Charles VIII's victory at the battle of Fournoue in 1495; Port de Bourgogne was dedicated to Prince Monseigneur le Duc de Bourgogne in 1757; Port de la Monnaie is less ostentatious; the Port d'Aquitaine is dedicated to the young duke of Aquitaine, Xavier de France, who died aged five months; Porte Dijeaux opens onto Place Gambetta. The Gross Cloche clock gate has two towers. The Bordalais have a great affection for its bell. The current one was cast in 1775 and is only rung on five days in the year to mark special occasions.

Bordeaux has no shortage of churches. The cathedral, Saint-André, is the most prominent. There has been a church on the site since AD814 and it was here that Louis VII, the then future king of France, married Eleanor of Aquitaine in 1137. It is 124m long and 23m wide. The two spires on the north facade rise to 81m. The royal door is renowned and its stained-glass windows are worth seeing. The Pey Berland tower is separate from the cathedral. You can climb its 231 steps for a view of the city and cathedral from this 15th-century tower. Basilique St Michel is the most visible church. You can see its spire from virtually everywhere in the city. The spire is separate from the church and known as Flèche St Michel (St Michael's arrow). It is the tallest church tower in southern France. Notre Dame, where the artist Francisco de Goya's funeral took place, is a hidden gem on the Place du Chapelet. It was built following the demolition of a Dominican monastery; the Dominicans relocated nearby and all that remains of the monastery are the cloisters in Cour Malby which you can visit. Other churches worth visiting include Basilique Saint-Seuring, Sainte-Croix, Our Lady's Church and Saint-Bruno.

The Place de la Comèdie contains two of Bordeaux's most impressive buildings: the Grand Théâtre and the Grand Hotel dating from the late 18th century. They form part of Bordeaux's golden triangle or the Quartier des Grands Hommes (the Great Men's Quarter).

Bordeaux's museums and art galleries offer an indoor alternative. The National Customs Museum on Place de la Bourse explores the development of customs through the centuries. The Musée des Beaux Arts in the Palais Rohan displays paintings from the 15th to 20th century; the Musée d'art

The Grand Hotel

Contemporain, in rue Ferrere, concentrates on modern art. The Centre Jean Moulin on the square of the same name commemorates the Resistance and deportations during the Nazi occupation. Other museums include Musée d'Aquitaine; Musée des Arts Décoratif et du Design; Cap Science Museum at Hanger 20; and Musée du Vin et Négoce, the wine and trade museum, not to be confused with the Cité du Vin focusing on the culture and life associated with wine.

Bordeaux's parks are pleasant places to find a shady retreat when hot. The Esplanade des Quinconces covers 12ha making it the largest city square in Europe. It takes its name from the quincunxes pattern of tree planting (a square with one tree in the centre). It is the location for circuses, fairs and outdoor events. The Jardin Public is a beautiful oasis away from the city's frenetic activity. It includes a herbarium, natural history museum and café. It is also the home of the Guignol Guerin puppet show. Le Park floral is beside the voie verte Bordeaux-Lacanau and close to camping at le Village du Lac. It covers 33ha and includes a lake, floral gardens, golf course and a stadium. Park aux Angéliques is on the right bank of the Gironde and has a cycle track, walks and picnic tables. This linear park gives excellent city views. The Jardin Botanique is also on the right bank.

The Gironde at Bordeaux is wide with a strong current and difficult to bridge. The first bridge, Pont de Pierre (Stone Bridge), was commissioned during Napoleon's reign and began construction in 1821. The bridge is constructed of pink stone and has 17 arches – one for each letter in the name

Napoleon Bonaparte. The bridge is the central fixture on the river. You get excellent views of the city and the river from it. The other bridges upriver from the Pont de Pierre are the Pont St-Jean and Pont François Mitterrand. Downriver is the recently built Pont Jacques Chaban-Delmas and the motorway bridge Pont d'Aquitaine. There is also a ferry service which crosses the river and goes to several stops downriver.

**Cycling the quays**

Cycling the quays affords an opportunity to see some of Bordeaux's more distant sights, cross the river by way of its newest and oldest bridges and gain a different perspective of the city from the opposite riverbank. The cycle of both riverbanks between the old and new bridge is approximately 8km in length.

Starting at the water mirror, cycle downriver towards Pont Jacques Chaban Delmas bridge along the quays mentioned earlier, passing restaurants and shops in the redeveloped docks. The cycle path is shared with pedestrians, so be careful. There are free Wi-Fi hotspots at points along the quay. The bridge is 2.7km from the centre. You pass close to the Cap Science just before the new bridge. The Cité du Vin is a few hundred metres beyond. This is a striking building shaped like a drunken wine glass. You must cycle on the road to reach it. To do so, cross a small bridge over the Écluses des Bassin à Flots. These in turn lead into the harbour where submarines were based during World War II.

The Cité du Vin explores the history and business of wine in the region. There is a charge to enter (€20 in 2018) so you need to allow time to get value for your visit. You should make sure that you lock your bike well and note that there are security restrictions on the type of bags you are allowed to bring in with you.

Cross the new bridge on either side depending on which view you prefer. You can now follow the quays on the right bank back towards the stone bridge. The park, le Parc aux Angéliques, is under development, on this bank. It is a linear park and you cycle beside it before taking a left and then right turn to cycle beside the road. The Jardin Botanique is on this bank, just off Allée Jean Giono. You will also see a Lion sculpture on your left as you approach the stone bridge. This is in Stalingrad square. You can return to the left bank by the stone bridge.

# PROLOGUE
*From Bordeaux to the Atlantic*

| | |
|---|---|
| **Start** | Le Miroir d'Eau (water mirror) |
| **Distance** | 135km |
| **Accumulated climb** | 220m |
| **Path** | Road and dedicated asphalt cycle path |
| **Map** | IGN TOP100 145 |

This optional stage is a 135km round trip visiting the Atlantic Ocean, west of Bordeaux. It follows the route of an old railway line which was asphalted over and turned into a cycle way. It passes through Bordeaux's outskirts, skimming around Bordeaux lake. It visits small towns and villages and travels through the wild and lonely forests of Les Landes (meaning heath or moorland) before reaching the Atlantic Ocean at the seaside town of Lacanau. The wildlife, both botanical and zoological, is rich and varied in the vast forest and the relatively poor and boggy soil. You may spot native red squirrels, martens, foxes, deer and wild boar as well as more common rabbits and mice. At night you will hear the whirring of nightjars and the hooting of owls.

If you prefer to break the route over two or three days, you could stay in Lacanau Océan or in the chambres d'hôtes near Salaunes – book in advance.

For the map showing the route leaving the centre of Bordeaux, see Stage 1.

◀ The prologue begins at the paddling pool, Le Miroir d'eau, in front of **Place de la Bourse**. Cycle downriver towards the sea – away from the stone bridge – on the riverside cycle path. There are stalls selling freshly squeezed orange juice here in summer and it is well worth trying. At H14 hangar building (easy to spot), 1.6km from the start, take the slope to your left to a cobbled area. Veer left and come to the main road running along the quays, **Quai des Chartrons**. Cross at the traffic lights and take the road straight opposite you, the Cours de Medoc. There should be cycle signs for Royan and Lacanau.

Use the cycle path on the right, most of which is separated from the road by kerb stones and paving, cycle through four crossroads and several other junctions to reach a large roundabout at **Place Ravezies**. Follow the cycle track as it veers to the right. ▶ Stay on the cycle path and cross two large roads and take the road following signs for Bordeaux lac. There are cycle signs for Royan and Lacanau. Use the cycle track that runs through the pavement. You reach a major junction 4.2km from Bordeaux centre with a cycle track to Bruges to your left. Cross the major road in front of you following the signs for Royan and Lacanau. The track is tree-lined in a few hundred metres.

The path splits. You take the left path for Lacanau. Turn immediately left beside a park. **Le Lac** is to your right with picnic tables and plenty of shade. You pass the entrance to the beach, a toilet block and the sailing centre. The path slopes right and passes under a motorway. Continue beside the motorway. This stretch is noisy but large concrete bollards separate you from the road.

The square is surrounded by large modern buildings.

*Cycle downriver along the quays*

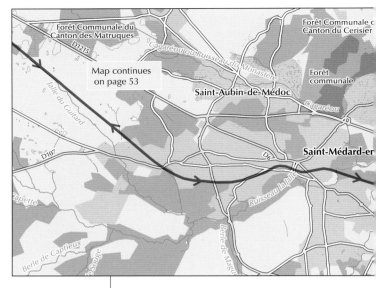

Map continues
on page 53

There is a sign for camping du Lac to the right. Cross a motorway slipway – there are no traffic lights. Then cross a major junction. Keep the motorway on your left. Pass under a road bridge following a sign for Lacanau (8.7km from Bordeaux). The path divides here. Turn left and cross a road (beside a roundabout) following signs for Lacanau–Océan (route no 1). ◄ The path runs beside a road.

*The path to the right, which you do not take, goes to Royan.*

The **Bordeaux to Lacanau railway** was built initially in the 19th century and stopped carrying passengers in 1954 and freight in 1962. The cycle track replacing the old railway line is categorised as a departmental road (D801) and thus is maintained to that standard. In essence it is a road from which motorised traffic is banned. There are plans to turn part of the track into a high-speed tram line – you will see signs protesting against this as you leave Bordeaux. So enjoy this route while you can.

48

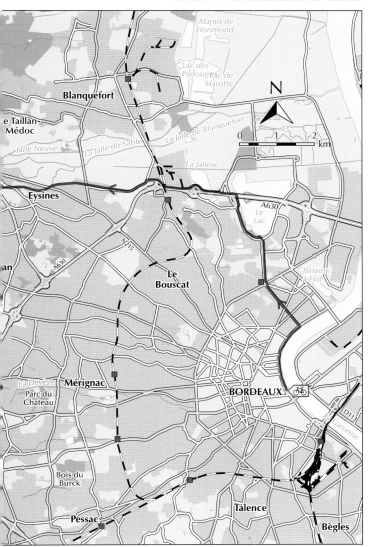

A sign for the town indicates you have reached **Eysines**. Cross a small road and then larger road and cycle past suburban houses. Reach a larger road where the path continues on the opposite side but slightly to the right. Pass under a road bridge 14km from Bordeaux centre. In 3km cross two busy roads with shops and a bistro on the corner of the second. Pass beside the bistro and later a chocolaterie, patisserie and boulangerie which also serves snacks. Cross another road and reach the old station at **St Médard-en-Jalles**, 18km from Bordeaux. There's a water tap, a toilet block and a small shelter.

The **station** has been converted into a restaurant. There is an old steam train, in a state of some disrepair, with a carriage behind stranded on a length of track outside the station building. It dates from 1913 and is a Couillet locomotive.

## ST MÉDARD-EN-JALLES

The town centre is 1km north of the station. It is suburban town with a rapidly growing population – currently around 28,000. It has restaurants, cafés, shops, a hotel and the usual other services.

Remains suggest that the town was occupied since Roman times. In the 17th century it became a centre for gunpowder production when six powder mills were established. These were not too successful: many explosions punctuated the early years of the mills' operations and one of the first owners of these mills, Monsieur Jéhan Dupérier, died in one. The state took them over on the owner's death and they were developed into a royal gunpowder factory. The town became a centre for military industry as a consequence and the tradition continues to this day. It is a centre for the nuclear weapons industry with the Centre d'Achèvement et d'Essais des Propulseurs et Engins (CAEPE), which develops and tests propulsion systems, being one of several defence companies based nearby. The town was also a centre for washerwomen who laundered linen from the hotels and big houses in Bordeaux.

The church in the town centre dates from the 11th century and is a national monument. It is dedicated to Saint Médard who was a bishop in Soissins in northern France but his following spread throughout the country. The bell tower dates from the 14th century and houses two bells cast in the 19th century. Graves of the Merovigian, the early Frankish people

*The town hall*

believed to be the first kings of France in the sixth, seventh and eighth centuries, were found in front of the church suggesting that it has been a religious centre from that time. The town hall is attractive with a small park close by. One of the town's more distinctive features is a large sculpture of a salamander, the town's emblem, on a grass patch between the church and the town hall.

Leave the station and follow the path past a fenced-off military zone with a road to your left. You continue through suburbs crossing small roads. The real forest begins 22km from Bordeaux. There's a sign for Salaunes (6km) and Lacanau Océan (44km).

The village, dating from the 16th century, has a church, shop and restaurant with a bar.

Cycle through pine forest with the occasional field or open space. Reach an oak glade with picnic tables and an old, but working water pump with the village of **Salaunes** on your right. ▶

There is a sign for Sainte-Hélène (5km) and Lacanau (38km) as you leave the village. Cross the D107E1 and skirt around a saw mill. Cross two further roads as the track straightens again. There are two chambres d'hôtes, 2km to the left from the next junction. There are no signs for these on the cycle track. Stelia Composites is on the corner at the next junction. There is a sign for another chambre d'hôtes, La Forestière, at the next junction. The path goes behind houses in **Sainte-Hélène** village nearly 34km from Bordeaux. Turn right to enter the small village with basic services.

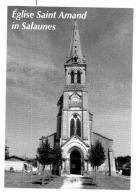

*Église Saint Amand in Salaunes*

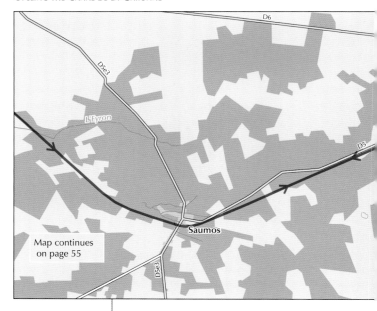

Map continues
on page 55

The path swings left. There is a public toilet with a tap and shelter in a green area. At the next junction there is a sign for Saumos (9km) and Lacanau (32km). Over the next 4km pass a Pension Cheveux and cross a largish drainage canal before arriving at **Saumos**.

The small village of **Saumos** has a simple church, Église Saint Amand, which dates from the 12th century. Its bell tower has space for two bells but there is only one. It was built on the Camino de Compostela pilgrimage route under the protection of the Knights Templar. There is shelter, tap, picnic tables and a children's play area. The station house, part of the old station, is private and in good repair.

Cross the busy D5 with care. The path runs alongside a canalette or drainage system called a *craste*. Pass signs

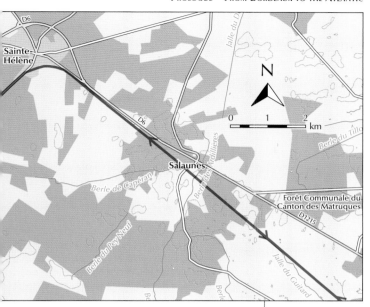

for Lacanau Ville (6km) and Lacanau Océan (19km) and then ride through an oak woodland with the Craste de l'Eyron to your left. There is a sign for le Porge at the next junction where you cross the busy **D3**. The signs show that you are within 2km of Lacanau Ville. ▸ Continue straight towards Lacanau and come to a bridge over the **Canal de la Berle**. Cross another bridge over a smaller *craste* and enter the town suburbs. There is a shelter in a grassy area beside a car park. Come to a sign for La Coustevre straight on, Lacanau Ville to the right and Lacanau Océan to the left. Here turn left onto Avenue du Lac to go towards Lacanau lake and Lacanau Océan.

There is a cycle track to the left in 1km (this is the D807 going to the Lege, Cap Ferret, le Porge and Arcachon Bay).

**Lacanau Ville** is a busy tourist town with supermarkets, shops, cafés, restaurants, laundrettes, etc. St Vincent's church is in a square opposite the town hall. The church was rebuilt stone by stone in the

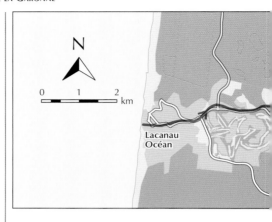

second half of the 18th century. The materials came from an old church in Talaris, which was threatened with flooding. The church has four gilded statues of St James, the Blessed Virgin and the child Jesus, Bishop Saint Valère and Saint Vincent. Lacanau is on the Compostela pilgrimage route. There is a toilet block to the right as you face the church opposite a restaurant.

Follow a busy road towards Lacanau Océan. Reach **La Bicyclette Jaune** (the Yellow Bike) restaurant. Turn sharp right – the route is still shared with traffic. The harbour is to your left and Lacanau lake beyond it. There is a large park with a beach, childrens' playground and trees offering shade to the left and holiday homes and camping to the right. In a kilometre take a cycle path to the left. (There is no sign on it.) In 100m see a sign for Lacanau Océan (11km) and Le Moutchic (6km). Cross a bridge over a river. Come to a T junction following signs as you turn left and then in 100m right. The road is wide but with little traffic. In 400m turn left onto a dedicated cycle track following the signs. This is a lovely stretch of mixed forest ending after 1.4km when the path runs beside the busy **D6**. Cross a large canal, **Canal des Étangs**, before

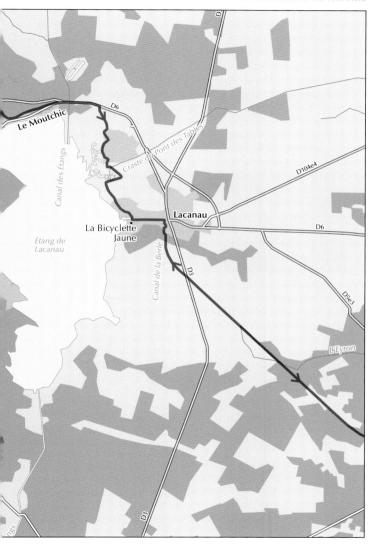

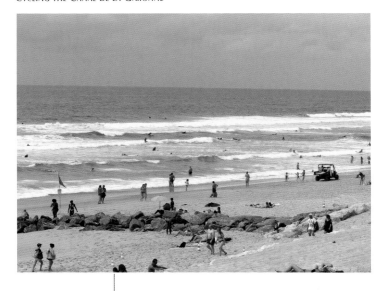

*The beach at Lacanau Océan*

This is a small holiday village with a hotel, restaurants, cafés, waterpark and camping in season.

Note a statue of a mariner on top of a tower on your left. He faces the Police Municipale station on your right.

a roundabout on the road beside you. Cross the main road at its exit from the roundabout. The path swings left and rises slightly. It joins a road (61.5km from Bordeaux) and **Moutchic village** is to the left. ◄ Turn right following signs for Lacanau Océan (5km) and le Huga (3km) onto the D801 dedicated cycle track. Pass through oak woods before rejoining pine forest. Pass under a road bridge in 700m and a couple of hundred metres later at a junction come to a sign for Lacanau Océan (4km) and le Huga (2km), both straight on.

Continue through trees beside a road gradually diverging from it. Cross a busy road and go through two pipe-like tunnels and cross another road. Veer right beside the D6 and follow the path beside the road until the two merge. ◄ There are public toilets on your right after a bus stop. Come to a roundabout. The ocean is straight ahead through a pedestrianised street. You are 67.5km from Bordeaux: reverse the route to return to Bordeaux.

## LACANAU OCÉAN

Lacanau Océan is a traditional seaside holiday town. It's busy and packed with visitors in summer. There are lots of new buildings, and shops, night-clubs, bars, cafés, restaurants, hotels, campsites and services. The beach is long and magnificent. Great waves roll in from the Atlantic making it popular with surfers. There is a surfing centre with a number of surf and kayaking schools. The tourist office is in the centre of the town in Place de l'Europe. A statue in the centre of the square created by a local sculpture, Dominique Pios, is entitled *Manueta la fille de l'alize et de la vague* (Manueta the daughter of the wind and the wave). It is an easy town to explore, the only difficulty being the crowds in high season. And this can come as a shock following the quiet of the forest.

Lacanau Ville and Océan are at the centre of a network of cycle paths and those interested may wish to explore more of the surrounding countryside. There is a path to Arachon Bay in the south and others to Maubisson, Cartens and beyond to the north.

*The main street in Lacanau Océan*

# STAGE 1
*Bordeaux to
Sauveterre-de-Guyenne*

| | |
|---|---|
| **Start** | Le Miroir d'Eau (water mirror) |
| **Distance** | 59.1km |
| **Accumulated climb** | 166m |
| **Path** | Asphalt and some road |
| **Map** | IGN TOP100 145 and160 |

This stage takes you out of Bordeaux city centre, your path following the river before climbing through small towns and villages. You follow a disused railway line now converted to an asphalted track as it snakes through woodland and vineyards passing old railway stations now converted to a variety of different uses. The track is named after Roger Lapépie (1911–96), a renowned professional cyclist from Bayonne in Aquitaine. It ends in the wonderful *bastide* town, Sauveterre-de-Guyenne.

Cycle to the stone bridge (upriver) from le Miroir d'Eau. Cross the river using the right-hand cycle track. The dome of St-Marie-de-la-Bastide is in front of you. You should see a sign for Sauveterre indicating right. Turn right, pass through a junction on the cycle track to join the Quai de la Souys. This long, straight dedicated track is reached 2.2km after leaving the paddling pool.

Watch out for **carrelets** on the riverbank among the trees to the right. These are traditional wooden fishing cabins and fishing nets built on stilts. Commercial fishermen use a square net which is winched into the water. They are privately owned and should not be visited without an invitation.

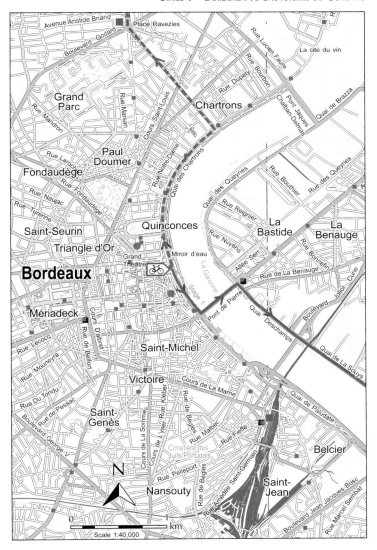

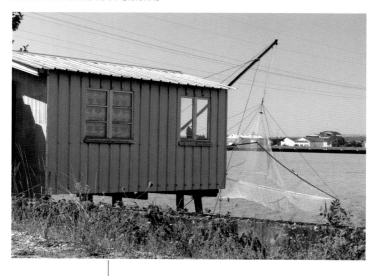

*Carrelets on the river*

Pass a sign for Floirac 3.9km from Bordeaux. Follow the cycle path and see a cycle sign for Creon 19km and Sauveterre 51km at 5.1km from Bordeaux. The path joins a small road where you cycle on the right and the traffic comes from the opposite direction. You soon revert to a cycle track. You will see chateaus set back from the road on your left including one listed as an historic monument. You leave the Gironde and taking a sharp left turn inland.

Latresne town's church spire is ahead. You reach a roundabout where the track crosses a road and continues towards the town centre. Join a busy road for a few hundred metres and look for a sign for a cycle track leading to the town centre which you follow. You cross another road, with a restaurant on the left, to reach the centre of **Latresne**, a pleasant small town with supermarkets, shops, restaurants, a hotel and its church, which dominates the town.

The path becomes wooded. You cross the Pimpine river and come close to it several times as you cycle the path. You enter the commune of Cénac. In under 3km

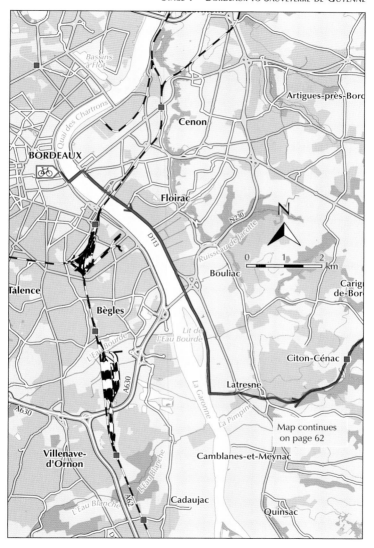

Map continues
on page 62

61

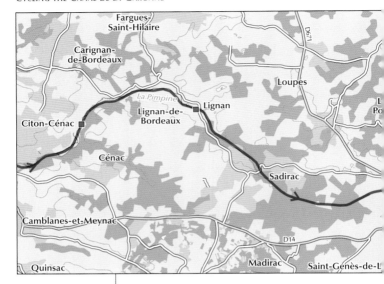

The car park here could be useful for those wishing to park and cycle part of the route.

you come to the first former station on the track: **Citon-Cénac**. It is now a gîte. Signs beside the station give the history of the railway and its stations. ◄

*The old station in Citon-Cénac*

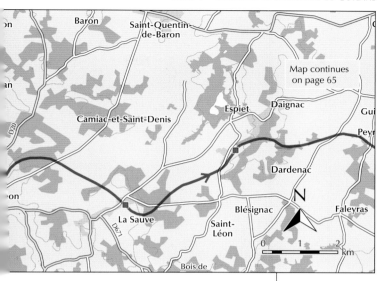

Map continues on page 65

Cross the road and continue for 3km before reaching **Lignan**. There is a shaded, grassy area just before you reach Lignan station with a good view of the church and a *lavoir* (wash-house) near a large house. There is also a picnic table under the trees. The station has been converted to a bistro: Bistrot de la Pimpine. This is very popular with locals and tourists alike. The church is St Eulalie and dates from the 12th century. Château de la Ligne is north of the town and offers luxury accommodation among its vineyards.

**Sadirac** is the next station, with a tap and picnic tables, just under 20km from Bordeaux. There's an old well close to it. The station houses the local heritage office for the Créon area. The area is a centre for making pottery using the local blue clay.

Continue on the path and within a kilometre come to a gate leading to the Velo Vert a Maison d'hôtes (B&B). An old bike leans against the sign. Pass through vineyards to reach **Créon**, in a little under 4km.

**Créon** is a small *bastide* town which is well worth a visit. It dates from the 14th century when Amaury III of Craon, with Edward II's authority, created a *bastide* in the middle of what was then forest. The town follows the traditional *bastide* design. There is a central square surrounded by arcades. The church, Notre-Dame, is on its corner – set back slightly. It dates from the 14th century but has been modified and developed over the centuries. It is well worth visiting.

The town has all of the usual services including a hotel on its outskirts. Créon station now functions as a tourist office. There are toilets, open during office hours, a picnic table and a tap. A cycling centre beside the station rents out bikes, tandems and ebikes. A bicycle shop in the town sells and repairs bicycles.

There's a lovely bridge over the cycle path after Créon station. Cross the D239 and reach **La Sauve station** boarded up, abandoned and graffiti covered.

## SAUVE MAJEURE ABBEY

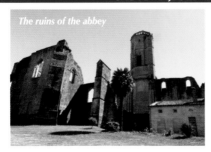
The ruins of the abbey

The ruins of the abbey, Sauve Majeure, are on the other side of Sauve village, approximately 1.5km from the cycleway. To reach it take the D239 southwest towards the village passing a school as it drops slightly. The abbey is easy to see as it is perched on a small hill. You pass the abbey walls, on your left, on what is now the D671. Note the Place St Jean on your left with the abbey above and the Restaurant de l'Abbaye facing onto it. Turn left just past this square onto Rue de L'Abbaye where the entrance is on your left.

The abbey was founded by St Gérald of Sauve Majeure in 1079. It was surrounded by a large estate of mainly forest – given to the saint by William

VII, Duke of Aquitaine. The buildings are considered excellent examples of Gothic and Romanesque architecture. There is an entry charge.

Continue on this rural stretch reaching a tunnel, originally built for trains, in a little over 3km. It is surprisingly cool when you enter and although lit it takes time to adjust to the darkness. Watch out for cyclists coming in the opposite direction.

Cross a road and note a large chateau on your right. There is a stone bridge, just under 2km from the tunnel. Reach **Espiet station**, now restored as a restaurant, with toilets beside the main building.

The path continues through woodland and in 4km crosses a road, turns left and then right to pass behind houses in the village of **Peyrefus**. The path nears Vincène stream shortly afterwards. **Bellefond** is the next village with its church on the hill. The path is exposed but

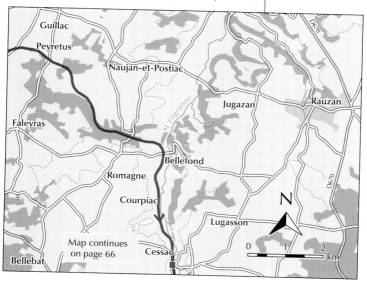

Map continues on page 66

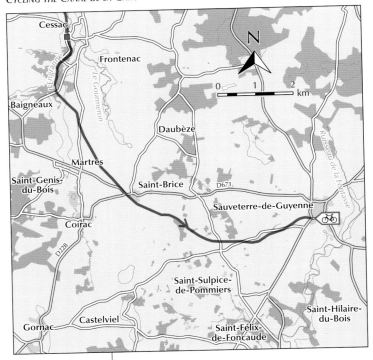

The village is a kilometre from the path and can be reached by turning left onto the D119.

you regain tree cover as you approach the village of **Frontanec**. Its station is relatively well preserved with a sign for the *lampisterie* (lamp store) and the *salle d'attente* (waiting room). ◄

Pass under a bridge with attractive metal railings. The path now runs through farmland with little shade. You soon see **Martres** church to your right. Continue towards **Saint-Brice**. There's a very busy crossing here and you should take care at the junction. Continue, passing through vines on both sides, before going under a bridge. You are now approaching **Sauveterre-de-Guyenne**. The path reaches the D672 and you see one of the gateways, Port la Font, into the town.

**Sauveterre-de-Guyenne** is an excellent example of an English *bastide*. Edward I founded it in 1281. Despite suffering during the Hundred Years' War, being captured and recaptured 10 times, it preserves its original grid layout. Arcades surround the main square. The church of Notre Dame at the square's edge dates from the 13th century but was extensively reconstructed in the 19th century following a fire and damage caused during the French revolution. The town has four gates; the Western gate, Port Saubotte, is the best preserved and can be visited to see its rooms and take in the views from the terrace on its top. Sauveterre has shops, restaurants, a hotel and some chambres d'hotes nearby.

*One of Sauveterre-de-Guyenne's half-timbered houses*

## STAGE 2
*Sauveterre-de-Guyenne to Marmande*

| | |
|---|---|
| **Start** | Porte Saint-Romain, Sauveterre-de-Guyenne |
| **Distance** | 41km |
| **Accumulated climb** | 209m |
| **Path** | Asphalt path and road |
| **Map** | IGN TOP100 160 |
| **Detours** | Bassane and the Moulin de Piis (3km); Meilhan-sur-Garonne (1.6km) |

This stage takes small roads through villages and hamlets to reach the medieval town of La Réole, a gem perched over the Garonne river and originally built by Richard the Lionheart. There are wonderful views over the plain through which both the river and canal pass. Descend from the town to reach the canal for the first time at Fontet. You have a choice of following the canal path to Castets-en-Dorthe, in the direction of Bordeaux, where the canal leaves the river Garonne. Alternatively, you can skip this and continue in the Toulouse direction. The stage ends in Marmande – an important town in the region dating from medieval times – famed as France's tomato capital.

There is a direct route from Sauveterre to La Réole (14km) following the D670. This can be busy with large trucks and cars travelling at speed. This guide gives an alternative route following smaller roads passing an attractive mill, chateau, small hamlets and villages.

Leave by the east gate, Porte Saint-Romain, and take the road (D670) following signs for La Réole, Agen and Monsegur as well as a blue motorway sign (A62). Pass the Cave de Sauveterre (wine producer) on the corner. After a kilometre cross a river, **La Vignague**, and come to Saint-Romain de Vignague. Take the second road (D230) to the left signposted for Castelmoron d'Albret, Caumont and Montségur among others. Cycle this for 700m and turn right at signs for St Martin de Lerm, 5km away on the D129. There is a sign for a voie vert towards Duras. The road goes through pleasant undulating countryside with a mix of vineyards, woodland and other agriculture. Carry on straight at a junction 3.4km from Sauveterre and do not follow the sign for a voie vert. In 500m follow the sign for **St Martin de Lerm** (the road to the left has signs for St Martin du Puy and St Léger de Vignague). Continue on the D129. You climb slightly and the road is exposed with neat well-tended rows of vines with good views on either side.

Pass through a hamlet, **Gabouriaud**, with a chambre d'hôte but nothing much else. Reach a T junction with the D15. Turn left following a sign for Mesterrieux and Landerrouet S/S. Cycle through **l'Épine** keeping an eye out for a crossroad where you turn right onto the D21 following signs for Saint-Sève (3.5km), Moulin de Loubens and Pont Eiffel. The D21 is the minor road at this junction. Continue straight ignoring signs for a voie vert. You come to a bridge over the Dropt river (9.5km from Sauveterre) with **Moulin de Loubens**, an old water mill, beside it.

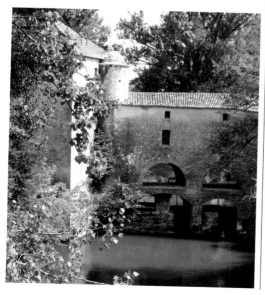

*Moulin de Loubens*

69

This bridge is the **Pont d'Eiffel**. It was commissioned by Baron Georges-Eugène Haussmann and designed and built by Alexandre Gustave Eiffel, a civil engineer and architect, best known for the Eiffel tower in Paris. It was completed in 1860 and restored in 1985. There is an old flour mill (*moulin*) visible from the bridge. This was built in the 14th or 15th century and was fortified and is now classified as a national monument.

Swing left, staying on the D21 following a sign for La Réole and Saint-Sève. The road climbs gradually to reach a crossroads with the **D126**. There is a sign for Loubens (0.5km) and Bagas (2km) to the right and one for La Violette (4.5km) to the left. Continue straight on the D21 in the direction of Saint-Sève (2.5km) and La Réole (6km). Climb through open countryside and note a tower ahead. This belongs to a chateau at the crest of the hill.

A large fort-like building, the **Château de Lavison**, is on the left-hand side of the road and there are outbuildings on the right. It dates from the 13th century. Edward III's eldest son, the Black Prince, used it as his hunting lodge. The chateau is now the centre of a thriving vineyard. It is possible to visit but it is best to book in advance.

The road drops down to cross a stream after a junction. There is a sign for Saint-Sève (0.5km) and La Réole (3.5km). Climb to reach **Saint-Sève**. The church is on the right when you come to the village and can be reached by taking the next turn. It is behind the Marie (mayor's office). The bell tower has two wooden shelters on each side.

The road undulates as you follow the D21 towards the D670 – the main road which you join at a junction in **Peyrefite**. Turn left, crossing this busy road and see a large sign for a roundabout; go through it taking the La Réole exit. Almost immediately pass a sign indicating that you are in **La Réole**. At the next roundabout take the exit

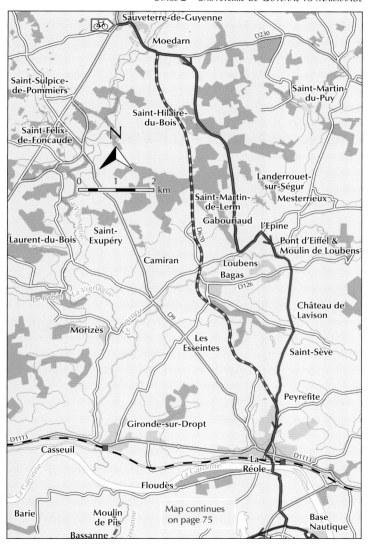

Map continues
on page 75

marked for La Réole (as well as the A62 and Agen). Follow the road, Avenue François Mitterrand, as it descends. Take a turn to the right with a sign for Centre Ville and the Office de Tourisme. This road, Avenue Carnot, leads to the town's main square, Place de la Libération.

Leave the town from Place de la Liberation. Take the road, rue des Freres Faucher, following signs for La Poste, Gare SNCF, Mijéma, Camping and Quais de Garonne.

## LA RÉOLE

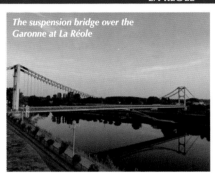

*The suspension bridge over the Garonne at La Réole*

La Réole has been a significant centre from medieval times and its buildings reflect this. The town's main attractions are close together and a signed walking route takes you to them all. The church of St-Pierre, and abbey beside it, are the town's best-known attraction. Built first in the 12th century it was nearly destroyed by the Huguenots, as was the priory during the war of religions. It was rebuilt in its current style in the 17th century. Its organ was taken and divided between the cathedral and a church in Bordeaux in 1812. It was restored in 2015. The church underwent further renovation in recent years but retains its earlier character. The abbey buildings have been converted for use as a museum, library and local administrative buildings. Nevertheless, you can walk around them. The staircases inside and the cloisters are worth seeing. There is a tremendous view over the Garonne river from the terrace beside the abbey buildings.

Richard the Lionheart built the old town hall, which is still intact. The aldermen's meeting room is on the first floor and is now used for exhibitions. The open-arched area beneath was a corn market. The Château des Quat'Sos is near the river. Louis VIII of France began its construction and Henry II of England completed it. The Black Prince's house, a private dwelling dating from the 16th century, was built far too late to have been his residence. This building, along with the 17th-century building Hôtel de Briet, are good examples of that period's architecture. The old lavoir du Cugey is also worth a look. Le pont du Rouergue, built in 1934 replacing a pedestrian one, is a 170m suspension bridge over the Garonne. There are good views of it from the terrace in front of the abbey and as you leave La Réole towards the canal.

The town has restaurants, chambres d'hôtes, shops, cafés, a hospital and a campsite (on the opposite bank of the Garonne river).

There is a slight incline and the road then swings left. Descend to a junction with a main road, 470m from the square. Turn right following signs for Bordeaux and Langon (D9E1). Take a sharp left to cross the suspension bridge with good views of the town on your right. Stay on the main road (D9E6) as it swings left and straightens. The entrance to the campsite is on the left. Swing right at a statue of the Blessed Virgin, Fontet Marie, and soon reach open countryside. ▶

Note the dark wooden barns.

Reach a junction with a main road 2.1km from the square and cross it with care going towards Fontet (0.7km). You will see a small sign for the voie verte beside the main signpost. Continue on this road, pass a sign for **Fontet** and reach a bridge, Pont Berrat, PK 182,762 – that is 182.762km from Toulouse – over the canal. Go over the bridge to cross to the cycle track on the opposite bank southern/left bank. ▶ The cycle track is categorised as a D road: D809.

Cross to the left bank.

You have a choice at **Fontet bridge** to either cycle to the start of the canal at the point where it leaves the Garonne river at Castets-en-Dorthe or skip these first 10km and carry on towards Toulouse. This guide covers the stretch to Castets-en-Dorthe for completeness and because there is plenty of interest along the canal's first kilometres.

The path is asphalt and easy to cycle but relatively exposed. Note the lovely dovecote, le pigeonnier de Lagrange, on your left. Pass under a bridge, carrying

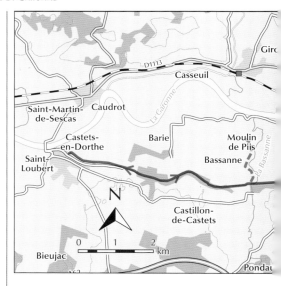

Cross to the north/
right bank.

the D9, and climb to the single-chambered lock/bridge
Écluse Fontet (49). ◄ Reach Pont de Loupiac (PK

Le pigeonnier de
Lagrange, near Fontet

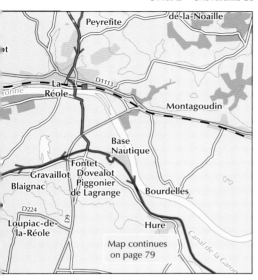

184,296) – the village of the same name is on the opposite bank. Continue on the north/right bank following a sign for Castets-en-Dorthe (9km), D809.

The path continues for an uninterrupted 1.2km stretch. The village of **Gravaillot** is on the opposite bank. ▸ The path comes to a junction with a larger road, D12, cross this with care. This is Pont de Gravilla. Pass under another bridge, Pont de Puybarban, a little over a kilometre further on. The next lock is Écluse (50) Bassanne with a small café and an old water pump.

You will see Saint-Saturnin's church spire on a hill above the village; the church's door is classified as a national monument.

### Detour to Bassane and the Moulin de Piis
Bassane is a small village between the canal and the river Garonne. Its Roman-style church, Saint-Pierre, dates from 16th century. The Moulin de Piis, on the village outskirts, dates from the 13th century. It is a 3km round trip.

Take the D266E1 north in the direction of the Garonne river: you will see the village and the church tower ahead, and in 600m you will reach a small

75

roundabout. The church is in front of you. It has a double bell tower with a covered wooden platform in front of it. To visit the mill, take the second exit from the roundabout signposted for La Réole and Moulin de Flaujagues. You skirt a cemetery wall. Watch for a minor road to the left just before a small bridge over the river Bassanne. There is a sign for Moulin de Piis at the road's edge. Follow this until it veers left. Leave the road and go straight, on a stony dirt track for 300m. The fortified mill is in front of you.

> The **Moulin de Piis** dates from the 13th century at least. It was owned by the same family until the French revolution when the owner was guillotined. The mill was restored extensively between 1999 and 2002. You will note a mill stone beside the door and the mill race to the rear. There is a sheltered picnic area – making it a good spot for lunch.

Retrace your ride to return to the canal at Bassane lock.

*Change to the south bank.*

Cross the bridge to the south/left bank and follow the canal path towards Castets. ◄ Both banks are wooded.

*Change to the north bank.*

Reach the Pont de Castillon in a kilometre and cross to the north/right bank of the canal. ◄ There is a sign for Castillon-de-Castets at the next bridge, Pont Noel. Pass under the Pont Hillon in 900m. Pont de Mazerac is the next bridge where you cross the D226 and continue on the same canal bank. You will note barges and other boats moored on the opposite canal bank as you approach the next bridge/lock, Écluse (51) de Mazerac. Cross to the

*Change to the south bank.*

south bank. ◄ There is a pizzeria nearby. The number of boats moored increases as you approach the next lock, 692m from Mazerac, Écluse (52) Les Gares. This is a single-chambered lock with a footbridge over it. Castets port is large with some beautiful old barges moored there. There is a water tap and a restaurant close by.

The path joins a road (D226) just before you reach Écluse (53) de Castets (PK 193). This is large-chambered

with a second lock gate beside it on its river side. It connects the Garonne river with the canal.

*A boat emerging from Mazerac lock*

The iron bridge spanning the Garonne in front of you is the **Pont Eiffel** although it was not either designed or built by Gustave Eiffel but instead was inspired by his work. It was built in 1905 and it is well worth climbing to see the bridge itself and the canal beginning. The bridge is encased in a metal framework and has separated pedestrian walkways on either side.

Climb from the bridge to enter the town centre of **Castets-en-Dorthe**.

The main attraction of **Castets-en-Dorthe** is its chateau which sits on a hill overlooking the Garonne valley and the canal junction. The town's name derives for Castets meaning castle while en-Dorthe probably refers to the wooden palisades which originally surrounded it. King Henry IV stayed there in 1585. The Protestant leader, Jean de Fabas, fortified it and made it his stronghold in the 16th century. It is possible to visit the castle and there is a small charge. It is open between Easter and All Saints' Day but you must arrange your visit in advance. It is known as either Château du Hamel or Château des Gots. There is a wonderful view over the valley from behind the village church.

Return to Fontet bridge by the same path. Remember to change banks at Écluse de Mazerac (51) to the north bank; Pont de Castillon to the south bank; Écluse (50) de Bassanne to the north bank; Écluse (49) de Fontet to the south bank.

## FONTET VILLAGE

The name Fontet derives from 'petite fontaine' meaning small fountain and the area has a number of wells and water sources. Its church, l'Église de Saint-Front, dates from the 16th century and is beside the canal at the bridge. It is not often open but if you peep through the keyhole you will see a plain church with a crucifix on the right, stained-glass windows and a chandelier. Take the road south to see the village. The dovecote, le pigeonnier de Lagrange, on your right is circular and topped with a dome. The village has a small *lavoir* on the right as you enter. The village bakery also sells some groceries. There are chambres d'hôtes here too.

One of Fontet's most distinctive attractions is found 400m along the canal towpath in the eastern direction. France has a history of eccentric museums in small towns and villages. Sadly, many have closed in recent years. Fontet has one of the best: the matchstick museum which celebrates model-making with matchsticks: le Musée d'Artisanat de monuments en allumettes et de Sciences Naturelles. Here you will see models painstakingly put together by Gerard Gergerès over the past 30 years including one of the Palace of Versailles. It also celebrates local life through pictures and exhibitions and is open in afternoons.

The cycle track passes under Fontet bridge and passes the matchstick museum in a typical black wooden barn on your right. You then arrive at the Base de Loisirs de Fontet (recreation centre), and **Base Nautique** (nautical centre) with swimming on the beach behind the centre, which is open in season for fishing and boating. There are spaces for camper vans, shaded picnic tables and a small café with a limited range of food on offer. Cycle around the base to reach the path on the other side.

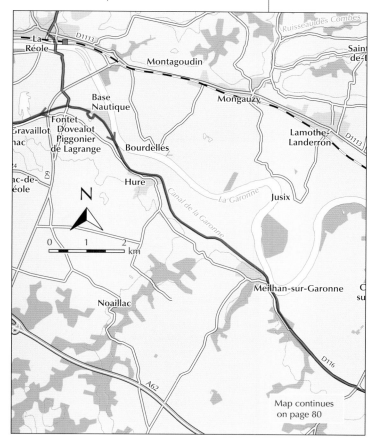

Map continues on page 80

*Moulin d'Auriole at the lock of the same name*

Trees shade the path for the next kilometre to Pont de Tartifume. Cross here to the north/right bank. ◄ The path runs between the Garonne river and the canal for a few hundred metres. The next lock, is Écluse (48) Auriole. Cross an overflow and note the imposing, modernised mill building, Moulin d'Auriole, dating from 1860. Continue on a shady path that leaves the river and pass under Pont Julian. A church spire comes into view as you approach the next bridge which leads to the village of **Hure**.

Change to north bank.

Pass under the bridge and continue on the well-shaded path to Pont du Lisos (PK 177,660). You leave the Gironde and enter the Lot et Garonne department in 500m. Pass a small memorial recalling a

drowning in 1946. Reach Pont de Pinayne (PK 176,520) in 100m and cross to the south side. ▶

Change to the south bank.

> In a woodland clearing, **Fontaine de la Font d'Uzas**, is a wickerwork sculpture of an American-style car named Eldorado: it represents the American dream and its impact on the world.

Emerge from the tree cover to reach the bridge at **Meilhan-sur-Garonne**.

**Detour to Meilhan-sur-Garonne**
The village is perched above the canal. To reach it, continue cycling on the road on the south/left bank of the canal. Pass a small restaurant across the road from the canal and turn sharply right to climb a steep 40m ascent to the centre. You reach the church of Saint Cibaird near the top of the hill. There are shops and a restaurant straight on and another restaurant on the ramparts to the right.

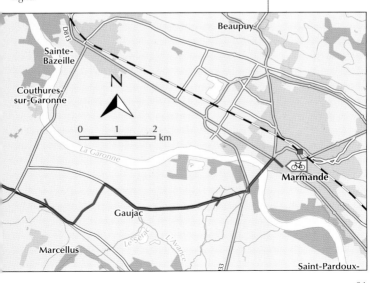

*Écluse des Gravières with a laitière at its side*

The village of **Meilhan-sur-Garonne** dates from the early 12th century when there was a church and a small abbey with some houses around it. King Henry III stayed in the castle in 1254. It changed hands during the Hundred Years' War. The English breached the ramparts in 1348 and the place where this occurred is known as the English breach. Edward of Woodstock, the Black Prince, stayed in the citadel in 1355.

There is an excellent panorama over the canal and the Garonne river from the Panorama de Tertre and there is a small harbour beside the bridge on the north/right bank with a shop/café and a tap. Behind this is a clean and tidy municipal campsite. There is also a bar/restaurant at the bridge on the north side but it is rarely open.

Retrace your route to the canal bridge.

The path changes to the north/right bank at the bridge. ▸ There are kilometrage signs for the towns ahead. Cycle between the canal and the Garonne river on your left. The D116 runs along the opposite bank. The next bridge/lock is Écluse (47) des Gravières. The lockhouse has a very pleasant *laitière* (dairy) selling ice cream and hot and cold drinks. They also rent some rooms.

Continue on the north bank passing under Pont de Cantis (PK 172,550) and Pont de Tersac where there is a picnic spot and a *relais* (meeting point) for cyclists. Note a *lavoir* and the École de Tersac (school) on the opposite bank. The path curves around a basin before crossing a busy road (D3) and reaching the lock/bridge, Écluse (46) des Bernès. Cross the narrow bridge over an outfall. Pass around a pipe crossing over the canal and come to Pont de Campot. There are fields of cereal crops to your left in summer. Pass under Pont de Marcellus (PK 169,150) and note signs for a voie vert to Marcellus, Gaujec (2.5km) and Marmande (8km). Bamboo plants narrow the path here. ▸ Take the Marmande path. Cross a main road and follow the VC4 to a T junction 1.8km from where you left the canal. Turn right onto the D116 following a sign for Gaujac and Marmande. You reach **Gaujac** in a kilometre.

> At the centre of **Gaujac** is the 19th-century Saint Paul's church. There is also an attractive water mill, Moulin du Pont, built by the Counts of Marcellus in 1685 on the Avance river (which you cross) beside the road. It was restored in the 20th century.

Stay on the D116 through flat open countryside for 1.8km passing under a six-arched railway bridge. Follow the road for a further 1.2km as it rises to a major roundabout. Take care going around this. Note a sign for a cycle track after the first exit (for the A62 motorway among others) and take this. It is easy to miss. Cycle beside the main road until you merge onto an unseparated cycle track and cross the suspension bridge. There is no cycle path across the bridge. Reach a main junction controlled by

Change to
north bank.

Leave the
towpath here.

traffic lights with a restaurant, Brasserie le Garonne, on the corner and turn right onto rue de la Libération following the signs for the Centre Ville and Marché. You will see a church in front of you and after passing this reach the Place du Marché which is at the centre of **Marmande**.

## MARMANDE

*Marmande has many half-timbered houses*

Marmande is justly famed for its tomatoes and is known as the tomato capital of France. However, you could also add prunes, peaches, tobacco and more recently kiwis to the crops for which it could also be renowned. It perches above the Garonne with an excellent view of the sweep of the river below.

Marmande was the scene of a massacre by the Crusader Army led by Prince Louis of France in June 1219. A report from the time records men, women and children being hacked to pieces until no one was left alive. Its position on the border between Guyenne and Gascon meant that it changed hands regularly between the English and French during the Hundred Years' War.

It became a communications centre in the 19th century with a river postal link to Toulouse, a Claude Chappe telegraph tower (automated semaphore system) and the arrival of the railway in 1855. The town is attractive with narrow streets and half-timbered houses and shops. Its ramparts are impressive. L'Église Notre-Dame dates from the 13th century. It is a beautiful church and despite renovations maintains the sense of a single designer. Its rose stained-glass window is well worth seeing. It also has a gilded wooden representation of Christ's burial, a painting of Saint Francis dating from the 17th century and an organ built by Cavaillé Coll in 1859. Its cloisters were added in the 16th century and the cloister gardens are classed as remarkable.

There is a gallery of sacred art beside the church (summer only). This displays paintings, sculptures and sacred objects such as monstrance. There is a bust of Saint Faustin from the 17th century, which was originally in Saint-Benoît's chapel. Saint-Benoît's chapel is at 91 rue de la Libération. Founded in 1645, it was a convent of the order of the Ladies of Saint-Benoît and was renovated in 1760.

There is much more to see in the town. The small streets clustered around the rue Labat have some lovely examples of half-timbered houses – although there are others scattered around the town centre. The town also has a modern quarter around Place Clemenceau with fountains and sculptures. A mosaic on the ramparts on Boulevard Richard Coeur de Lion depicts the town's history.

Le tour du Passeur is a watchtower with excellent views of the Garonne river below. The Jardin des Sources (Garden of the Springs) is tucked away from the town, with streams, wooden bridges, shade and picnic tables. It is a good place for a picnic or a ramble. Watch out for snakes though. There is a large park beside the river, Parc de la Filhole. It has horse riding, basketball, football, playgrounds, a stopping point for camper vans, river fishing and a beach among other things. Finally, the suspension bridge over the Garonne dates from 1932. It replaced an earlier one which was built in 1838.

The town has all the usual facilities. It has a train station and is on the Bordeaux to Toulouse line.

**STAGE 3**
*Marmande to Buzet-sur-Baïse*

| | |
|---|---|
| **Start** | Marmande suspension bridge |
| **Distance** | 40.4km |
| **Accumulated climb** | 102m |
| **Path** | Asphalt and some road |
| **Map** | IGN TOP100 60 |
| **Detours** | Tonneins (12.7km); Aiguillon (12.6km) |

This stage follows the canal as it wends its way through lush farming countryside. Mas-d'Agenais is one of the oldest and most interesting villages on the canal. Its main attraction is a Rembrandt painting of Christ's crucifixion in the village church. There is a detour to Tonneins, an old town on the Garonne and once the capital of France's tobacco industry. You pass the black wooden *séchoirs*, barns used for drying tobacco; some of them are still in use. The ride includes a trip around the perimeter of the nature reserve at Mazière Lagoon and a detour to Aiguillon where the Lot river enters the Garonne. The stage finishes in Buzet-sur-Baïse, on the Baïse river, another part of the river network intersecting the canal. Buzet is an important wine-producing region whose wines are highly regarded worldwide.

There are two options to reach the canal. To cycle the full canal return to the point you left it on the previous stage. For the shortcut, follow the busy main D933.

◀ Re-cross the suspension bridge and cycle on the D933E1 to the roundabout ahead. Take the second exit marked Gaujec (D116). Pass under the arched railway bridge; cycle through **Gaujec** with the mill and church on your left-hand side. Keep an eye out for a small sign for Marcellus (2.5km) on the VC4 to your left just over a kilometre from Gaujec church. Take this turn and cross the main road (**D143**) when you reach it and descend to the canal towpath. Make sure to cycle in the direction of Toulouse – that is turning left when you reach the canal at Pont de Marcellus.

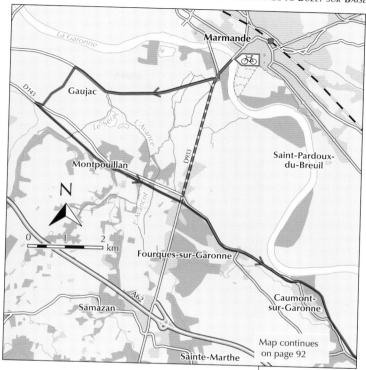

Marmande

La Garonne

D143

Gaujac

Le Serac

L'Avance

Montpouillan

Saint-Pardoux-du-Breuil

D933

N

L'Avance

0   1   2
        km

Fourques-sur-Garonne

A62

Samazan

Caumont-sur-Garonne

Sainte-Marthe

Map continues on page 92

## Shortcut via the D933

Re-cross the suspension bridge and cycle on the D933E1 to the roundabout. You need to go through this and take a cycle track that goes under the roundabout. Follow this in the direction of the A62. The cycle track runs for most of the 4.5km to the canal. There is a roundabout after a petrol station. Take the second exit and the bridge over the canal is ahead of you. Cross to the southbank to reach the towpath.

From Marcellus bridge (PK 169,150) continue on the tree-lined path and reach Pont de Baradat in 800m. The

87

*A séchoir for drying tobacco*

path drops below the canal but rejoins it at Pont de Rayne which you pass under.

**Barns** of one type or another are scattered over the countryside between Marmande and Agen; note the interesting wooden building on the opposite bank. Most of these were originally *séchoirs*, drying houses for tobacco leaves. Tobacco is still grown locally and you can see it drying in either the traditional *séchoirs* or in polytunnels.

After Pont Larouquière (PK 166,350) pass under a railway bridge and come to a cycle meeting point: point relais voie verte Montpouillan. The next lock is Écluse (45) de L'Avance. Change here to the south/left bank. ◄ There is a double-arched aqueduct over the

*Change to the south bank.*

88

Avance river immediately after the lock. You can see carp swimming in the river and you may spot kingfishers flashing along its banks.

Pass under Pont des Sables and reach Fourques-sur-Garonne harbour. ▶ The harbour is a centre for aquatic sports and boat hire. There's a café with ice-cream on sale. There is also a restaurant close by (in season).

Pass under Pont de Marescot (PK 163.540), climb back to the bridge and cross to the north/right bank. ▶ This is not well signposted and be careful joining the road. Descend and re-join the canal towpath. There is a village, **Fourques-sur-Garonne**, on the opposite (south) bank, at Pont de Fourques. Cross the bridge if you wish to visit: there is a small shop and a cycle meeting point with picnic tables.

Continue on the north bank and come to a monument on your left.

The **monument du Vapeur du Gascon aux Alotimes** commemorates a tragedy that occurred in 1908. One of the few steam barges that ferried up and down the canal exploded killing its crew members. Fellow sailors erected the monument in the year following the accident. There is an attractive old outbuilding on the opposite bank just after the monument.

Pass under Pont de l'Église de Fourques and then cross a small concrete spillover. Go around a small port area after the Pont de Caumont (PK 160,305). The path joins a road briefly and continues on the north bank. **Caumont-sur-Garonne** is over the bridge and has some fine buildings. ▶ Cross a road at the next bridge, Larroque. The path drops to the wheat field level, below the canal but rises to the canal level in 700m. Cross a sluice bridge, merge with a road again for a few metres before passing under Pont de Larriveau (PK 156,945). The path veers left a kilometre from the bridge before you climb to the bridge/lock, Écluse (44) de Mas-d'Agenais and the notable village of **Mas-d'Agenais**.

This is where you re-join the canal if you choose to take the D933 from Marmande.

Change to the north bank.

There is a vast cereal monoculture on your left.

## MAS-D'AGENAIS

*Mas-d'Agenais's covered marketplace*

A visit to the welcoming village of Mas-d'Agenais is recommended. It was an important river crossing point and a toll bridge, across the Garonne, was built in 1840 and renovated and upgraded in the 20th century. Bicycles have been turned into ornaments and line the route from the canal to the village.

The church, Église Saint Vincent de Mas-d'Agenais, was built between the end of the 11th century and the beginning of the 12th century. There are Romanesque capitals showing scenes from the Old Testament. The wooden choir was carved for the Benedictine Abbey in La Réole. The highlight of a visit here however is to see Rembrandt's painting of Christ crucified, dating from 1631. This was originally part of a series that Dutch Prince Frédéric-Henri of Orange-Nassau commissioned. It was bought at an auction in the 19th century and made its way by devious routes to the church.

Brick ramparts surrounded the village in medieval times. Mas had five gates of which only one remains – attached to a small castle. The castle was demolished in the 17th century and some of its beams were used to build the grain market in the main square. The village has a five-sided *lavoir* supplied with water from the Galiane source.

The Mas-d'Agenais and Sénetis forest is 2km southwest of the village. This covers 730ha and is easily accessed by the D6, although the A62 passes through it and most of it is on the southern side of that motorway.

The towpath continues on the north bank passing behind the boat hire company's (Le Boat) offices, with a meeting point for cyclists beside the offices. There is a small takeaway here and the Le Boat shop sells drinks in season.

You now cycle close to the Garonne river – on your left. Pass under the suspension bridge which spans both the canal and the Garonne and reach Pont de Lagruère (PK 153,315) with a shaded picnic area beside the river. Climb up, join the road for 10m and then rejoin the cycle path. You reach the next bridge in 1.1km. Climb to the road, the track veers around a restaurant and a *halte nautique* (mooring for boats). Behind the restaurant is a small park, Parc de retour aux sources, which allows visitors and school groups to explore the natural world through their different senses. There is a small campsite with toilets open in season.

## Detour to Tonneins and Parc Naturelle de l'Étang de la Mazière

▶ Take the road on the north/right bank from the *halte nautique*. There is a sign in the opposite direction for Calonges. The road is parallel to the canal for 100m. It turns left crossing a small bridge and goes through large fields of cereal until, after a kilometre, you reach a crossroads at **Saint-Juin**. The ruins of the church are on your left, its bell-tower still standing with space for two bells.

The road (C2) signed for Tonneins passes a gravel works on your left, la Farge Granulats Sud. Continue on the main road veering right at a fork with a small road to the left to reach a crossroads with the main **D234**. Cross this and take the small road opposite going towards the Garonne. It swings right and straightens until you reach a T junction with the river directly in front. Turn right and cross a bridge over the l'Ourbise, a Garonne tributary. Reach the main road (4.8km from the canal), and turn left crossing the main road. There is a restaurant/creperie here. Cross the bridge in front of you with the town and its ramparts to your right. You are now in **Tonneins**. The quays are on your right. Carry straight on, climb a slight incline and turn right following a sign for Centre Ville onto the Cours de la Marne. Reach a square on your left, at the other side of which is the church of Notre Dame. Continue to Place Jean Jaurès, formerly Place du Château. There is a terrace on the right with a panoramic view over the river.

There are shorter routes to Tonneins further along the canal towards Toulouse. This one is selected for its rural scenery and its access to a large nature reserve.

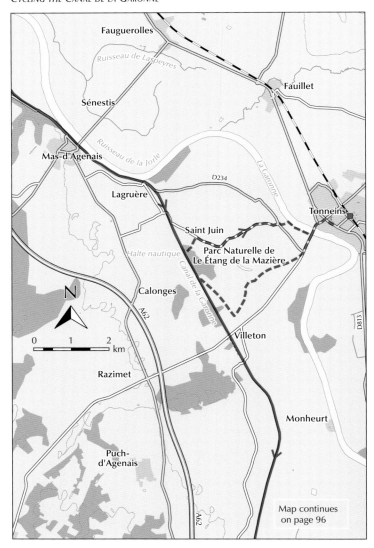

Fauguerolles

Ruisseau de Laspeyres

Fauillet

Sénestis

Ruisseau de la Jorle

La Garonne

Mas-d'Agenais

D234

Lagruère

Tonneins

Saint Juin

Parc Naturelle de
Le Étang de la Mazière

Halte nautique

Canal de la Garonne

N

Calonges

A62

0  1  2
km

Villeton

D813

Razimet

Monheurt

Puch-
d'Agenais

A62

Map continues
on page 96

## TONNEINS

Tonneins was France's tobacco capital until 2004 when its factory closed. In its heyday, barges carried tobacco from the quays below the town for distribution in France and worldwide. France is still the world's fifth largest tobacco producer but this is nearly all exported to developing countries as Europeans prefer a different tobacco taste.

Tobacco-growing dates to the latter years of the 16th century. A royal factory was established in 1721 and at its peak employed 1200 people. The town suffered an economic decline following the factory's closure as it resulted in over 500 redundancies – a significant number in a town with a population of 10,000. However, there has been a regrowth in the production of tobacco and another crop, hemp, which was traditionally produced in the area. Farmers grow newer crops such as kiwis and you see their vines as you cycle to and from the canal.

Tonneins is a very typical French town and gives the visitor the opportunity to experience everyday life. Éspace A Garonna de Tonneins, on the Quai de la Barre, is a museum with exhibitions on the town's crafts and industry.

The return to the canal takes a different route. Recross the bridge over the Garonne and continue on the busy main road passing the turnoff for the D234 with signs for Lagruère (Halte Nautique) and Mas-d'Agenais.

*Tonneins on the banks of the river Garonne*

Continue on the D120 and in 20m take a right turn signposted (small sign) for Réserve Naturelle de l'Étang de la
Mazière – 1km from Tonneins centre. Cycle on this road,
chemin du Barrat, through maize and sunflower fields
and in 900m come to a noticeboard describing the flora
and fauna found in the reserve.

## NATURE RESERVE – MAZIÈRE LAGOON

The reserve aims to preserve the bio-diversity of an area that is farmed with
increasing intensity. Established between 1969 and 1974, it was decreed a
reserve in 1985. It initially covered 68ha but further parcels of land were
added to reach its current size of 102ha. It is an important area for both resident and migrating species. Scientists working there have recorded:

* 50 species of mammal including nine bat species
* 12 amphibian and six reptile species
* 244 bird species
* 47 dragonflies or damselflies (Odonata) species
* 13 fish species
* 356 plant species
* 1000 other insect species.

The species found here include otters, martens, the European pond tur-
tle, black kites, kingfishers, wrynecks and nightjars among the vertebrates. The
reserve is studying the use of dragonflies and damselflies as indicator species
of environmental quality. There is an active bird-ringing programme on the
reserve for both resident and migrating species. Visitors must arrange visits in
advance and given the importance and fragility of the reserve these must have
a guide. Visit the website: www.sepanlog.org/reserve-naturelle-de-la-maziere
for more details. Follow the signs for the reserve offices and buildings.

Continue on the same road and note a hut beside the
road with panels giving further information on the area
and on the Ferme de la Grande Mazière – a typical example of a traditional farmhouse. Reach a T junction (4.3km
from Tonneins centre) and turn right. Pass through kiwi
plantations, with traditional tobacco drying barns along
the way. The canal is to your left and you can rejoin it at
several points. A small road to the left leads to Écluse (43)

de la Gaulette and you can join the canal path there. To head towards the *halte nautique* keep on the road veering left beside the canal and come to a bridge (PK 151.050) and join the canal path here. Turn right if you wish to go back to the *halte nautique*, turn left if you want to skip these 1.2km.

**Main route continues**

From the *halte nautique* pass under a bridge at (PK 151.050) and in 2km arrive at Écluse (43) de la Gaulette. There is a small harbour at the next bridge, le Pont Canal (also known as Pont la Barth) in **Villeton**. ▶ Cross the D120 and continue on the north/right bank to the next lock/bridge, Écluse (42) de la Gaule. The path is shaded as you pass three bridges – Monheurt, Vigneau and Morin – to reach the next lock/bridge, Écluse (41) Berry, which is 4.7km from the previous lock, La Gaule. A small channel bypasses the lock on your left. Pass behind the lock house and ride through intensively farmed land after Pont de Lompian. The path is tree-lined and you may see some large silos on the opposite bank shortly after the bridge. **Damazan** (PK 140) is the next important town on the canal. There is a small port and a meeting point for cyclists. Climb to the main D8E1 road.

The town hall is beside the bridge; a pizzeria, a small museum celebrating rural life and a toilet block are close by.

## DAMAZAN

The town's ramparts, with a turret at their end, are the first thing to strike you as you cross Buzet bridge. The main road swings around the east of the old town but the centre is easily accessed by taking any of the small roads to your right.

Damazan traces its foundation to 1259 when the Count of Poitiers and brother of King Louis of France ordered its construction. It was built according to the *bastide* design but with fortifications and a moat. It changed hands through the Hundred Years' War and the English crown controlled it for long periods. Its central main square is its primary attraction. The town hall is in the square's centre while arcades surround it. While the town hall dates from the 19th century, the staircase to the side dates from the 14th century and there is a well opening behind the building.

The arched area underneath the town hall is still used as a market place. The square has shops and a café. Attractive half-timbered houses face the square and can be seen around the town. Notre Dame church, just off the main square, was rebuilt in the 16th century.

There are cafés, restaurants and shops in the modern town. The campsite, Camping du Lac, is outside the town, off the D108 in the direction of Buzet-sur-Baïse. Unusually, Damazan has its own cricket club, the DCC. Its ground is near the campsite beside the lake.

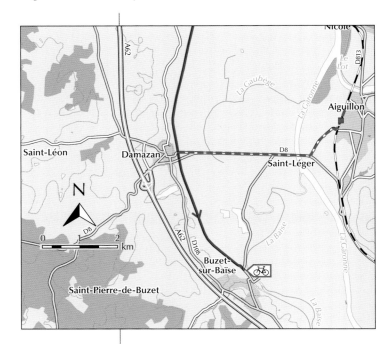

**Detour to Aiguillon via Saint-Léger**
To visit Aiguillon, take the D8E1 north from the canal. Join the main **D8**. Pass a petrol station and reach a junction with the main road. Take care as you cross to the right-hand side. This road is very busy but there is a hard

shoulder. Pass a fruit farm on your right and then pass over the Baradasse river. After 3.4km from the bridge at Damazan bridge you reach **Saint-Léger**. There is a chambre d'hote on the right, Château de Grenier, close to the village church. Cross the bridge over the Garonne, the Pont de Saint-Léger. ▶ In 100m turn left on a road signposted for Aiguillon (D642). The town's church spire and chateau are clearly visible and this is the best overall view. Swing right at a junction and pass under a railway bridge and turn left still following a sign for Aiguillon. Climb to Allée Charles de Gaulle and follow the signs for Centre Ville to reach the Place de XIV Juillet. The old town is easily explored from here as the old streets are in front of you.

The bridge, built in 1935, is narrow with heavy traffic.

*A half-timbered house in Aiguillon*

**Aiguillon** is a small town on the right bank of, and overlooking, the Garonne. It derives its name from the Latin *aculeus*, which refers to the confluence of the Garonne and the Lot close by. It was an English town from the 13th century and was fought over during the Hundred Years' War. Duke Emmanuel-Armand de Vignerod (1720–88) was one of King Louis XV's ministers and he began a development that shaped the town. The town centre was cleared to make way for his chateau, Château des Ducs. It was converted to a school in 1965 – Le Collège et le Lycée Stendhal – and it continues in the same role. Saint-Felix's church stands in Place Clémenceau. Aiguillon has a railway station, shops, restaurants, chambres d'hotes, a bicycle repair shop and campsite.

Return to Damazan by the same route following the D8 and then the D8E1 to the canal.

After crossing the D8E1, descend onto a small road shared with cars. Pass under the D8 bridge and 400m from Damazan take the cycle track to the right and continue on a path shaded by trees. Climb and descend over Pont du Doux and then Pont de Burenque where the canal widens on both sides. Shortly after this, the path is shared with cars. Reach a *halte nautique* with a restaurant, Au Bord de l'Eau, where the path skirts the mooring. This is part of the Buzet port. The path now runs beside a main road but is separated from it by a metal barrier and curb stones. The bridge at **Buzet-sur-Baïse**, just over 4km from Damazan, is ahead of you. ◀

Note the disused factory to your left, Cellulose du Buzet, and a large weir.

## BUZET-SUR-BAÏSE

The site of the town has been occupied from prehistoric times. The present town grew up around the chateau of the same name, which dates from the late 10th century. The current building was built in the 11th century by Sanche Guillaume, Duke of Gascony. The English burnt down the castle in the 13th century but it was rebuilt using the original foundations. The

The chateau in Buzet-sur-Baïse

Noaillan family took it over in the 15th century. It changed hands through marriages and other events over the centuries. All the time it was added to and embellished. Dr Michel Demangeat, a renowned Lacanian psychoanalyst practicing in Bordeaux, bought the chateau and its grounds in 1981 and used it as a holiday home until his death at the age of 83 in 2011. He invested significantly in the chateau's maintenance and renovation. His son, Olivier, sold the contents in 2017. The future of the chateau itself is uncertain. It is a national monument despite being privately owned and is not open to the public. You can see it in the distance, perched on a hill, from high ground behind the town church. The D108 in the direction of Ambrus and Xaintrailles goes close to it and, once you pass under the A62 motorway, gives a good view of its towers from different angles.

Buzet is a major wine-producing centre dating from Roman times. In the mid-19th century, phylloxera blight severely damaged the Buzet wine business. Wine producers came together to fight a nearly 100-year decline and formed the cave coopérative in 1953. It gained l'Appellation d'Origine Controlée (AOC), Côtes de Buzet in 1973 changing to AOC Buzet in 1986. The co-operative has sought to make its business more environmentally friendly and sustainable since the beginning of this century and has achieved certification for quality management and sustainability. Four of its wines are bee-friendly and hives are installed in their vineyards, part of measures taken to increase and protect bio-diversity in its vineyards. Vegan, low-alcohol and organic wines are produced, and it is possible to visit the cellar and taste the wines at 56 Avenue des Côtes de Buzet.

There is an excellent restaurant, Auberge du Goujon qui Frétille, on the town side of Buzet, a chambre d'hôte closeby, plus restaurants, shops and other services in the town.

## STAGE 4
*Buzet-sur-Baïse to Agen*

| | |
|---|---|
| **Start** | The canal bridge in Buzet |
| **Distance** | 30.6km |
| **Accumulated climb** | 50m |
| **Path** | Asphalt cycle path with some road |
| **Map** | IGN TOP100 160 |
| **Detours** | Bruch (3.8km); Sérignac-sur-Garonne (1km) |
| **Excursions** | Port-Sainte-Marie and Clermont-Dessous (20km); Nérac (30km) |

This short stage takes you through countryside typical of the route. It starts at an important point, the junction with the Baïse river. The path continues through the Garonne plain with views of the hillside Clermont-Dessous church in the distance. There are detours to two lovely towns: Bruch and Sérignac-sur-Garonne. The final stretch takes you across one of the highlights of the whole route: the aqueduct over the Garonne just before Agen, an engineering triumph. Agen's old quarter contains excellent examples of medieval buildings and more sights can be visited by taking one or both of the excursions. One excursion visits Port-Sainte-Marie and Clermont-Dessous – towns overlooking the Garonne, and the other takes in Nérac, a medieval town on the Baïse river.

Take the path from Buzet bridge towards Agen and Toulouse on the north/right bank. Curb stones separate it from the road. There is a road straight in front with a no entry sign. Follow the path to the left and enter the port area by a road yielding to any traffic. Cycle around the port passing a dry dock on the right. Pass car parks, a picnic area and open space. The building to your right houses the port offices. There is a shop, café, etc, with toilets at the side. Follow the road as it swings sharply left to the double chambered lock connecting the canal to the Baïse river. The bridge carrying the road is between the two lock chambers. Turn right towards the canal and

**Buzet port**

follow the road for 1.5km. This is shared with cars. Écluse (40) de Larderet is the first lock/bridge after Buzet harbour (3.5km). Cross here to the south/left bank. ▸ The canal widens into a small basin between this and the next lock 220m away, Baïse (39) lock. Tree branches partially obscure the lock sign. A three-arched aqueduct takes the canal over the Baïse river. You should dismount or keep a foot on the path to cross this rough, cobbled path. The motorway is close by on the right.

Change to the south bank.

Pont de Thouars (PK 130.72) is 5.3km from Buzet. Pass under the bridge (keeping to the right), then 1km later under a railway bridge and then under Pont de Feugarolles. Pass silos on your right before passing under two road bridges. Signposts immediately to the right are for: Feugarolles (1km), Saint-Laurent (4km) and Port-Sainte-Marie (4.5km). ▸

This route to Port-Sainte-Marie is on a very busy road (D930) without a hard shoulder and not recommended.

Continue on the south bank passing under Pont de Castelvieil (PK 128,775) a little over 7km from Buzet. There is a chateau of the same name (also spelt Castelbeil) to the south. The path joins a road

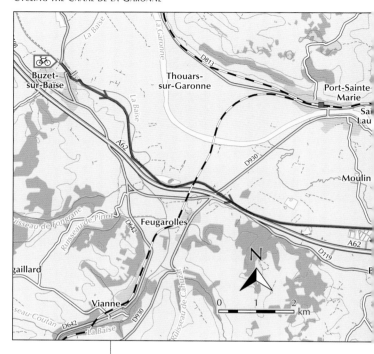

Excursion 1 to Porte-Sainte-Marie and Clermont-Dessous starts from here.

Excursion 2 to Nérac starts from here.

and climbs to the next bridge, Pont de Thomas. ◄ As you cycle this relatively exposed stretch, visible in the distance to your left is the church, St John the Baptist, Clermont-Dessous. There is a sign for gîtes at the Moulin St Laurent at the next bridge, which also offers B&B and camping. Fruit cultivation dominates the opposite canal bank. There are button-controlled traffic lights at the next bridge/lock, Écluse (38) l'Auvignon, regulating cars crossing the bridge and those cycling on the towpath. ◄ There is a long overflow around the lock and herons frequent its channel. There are signs for St-Laurent (3.5km), Porte-Sainte-Marie (4.0km), Bruch (1.5km) and Nérac (12km).

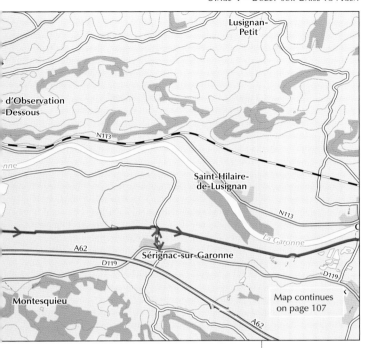

Map continues
on page 107

### Detour to Bruch

Leave the path and head south for Bruch. Cross the bridge over the motorway. You will see a large tower to your left. Reach a busy main road 1.4km from the canal. Cross this with care. Immediately, come to a second road. Turn left. The tower is in front of you. The ramparts are on your right as you cycle. Enter the village through the old town gate.

> **Bruch** is a gem. Barely mentioned in guides, it has excellent examples of buildings from the Middle Ages. It dates back to early Roman times but work on the present-day village began in the 10th century with the construction of a moat and wooden tower.

*The clocktower
in Bruch*

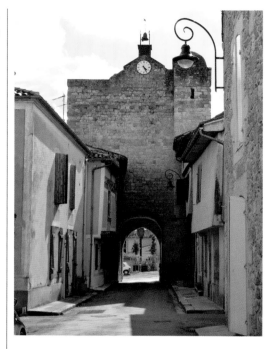

The village has a grid layout. The streets were divided according to guilds or trades with a shop on the ground floor and with the upper storeys overhanging the street. These half-timbered houses date from the 15th and 16th centuries. The gate tower nearest the canal is very impressive. The second gate is on the side away from the canal and is set into the walls. The old covered marketplace, remaining ramparts and half-timbered houses on narrow streets give a sense of what the village was like in medieval times. The church is on the town's outskirts on the road towards Nérac.

Take the same route back to the canal.

Cross an aqueduct over the l'Auvignon river. Pont de Page (PK 124,410) is next followed by La Pougnang and de Frècac. There is a sign for Montesquieu, 2km away. ▸

Change to the north bank here. ▸ The path joins a small road so watch for traffic. There is a chambre d'hôte on the left before Pont de Menote (PK 121,090). This stretch runs beside orchards and other intensive fruit production. There are large silos to your left. The canal widens into a small harbour before the next bridge leading to Sérignac-sur-Garonne.

**Detour to Sérignac-sur-Garonne**

This small town is south of the canal. Cross the bridge and follow the tree-lined road straight for a few hundred

Change to the north bank.

Montesquieu has a panoramic view and medieval ramparts, it also gave the writer, Montesquieu (1689–1755), his name.

*Part of the aromatic garden in Sérignac*

metres. The tourist office is the first notable building that you see. Carry straight on to the small street in front of you to explore the centre.

> **Sérignac** was originally a Gallo-Roman settlement but retains many medieval structures. Its church, Notre Dame de Sérignac, dates from the late 12th and early 13th centuries. Its bell tower, hexagonal in shape, was built two centuries later behind the church.
>
> The main street is partially arcaded with both wooden and stone buttresses. The houses are half-timbered and excellent examples of their type. There are several manorial houses in the village. Le manoir de Menjoulan faces onto the main D119. It was built in the 17th century and retains many of its original features including a dovecote. A large dovecote such as this was an indicator of wealth as the droppings were collected and used as fertilisers. The manor is now a hotel and restaurant named 'Le Prince Noir'.
>
> There is a small supermarket/tabac/bakery on the D119 and a pizzeria in the centre. Aside from the hotel, there are chambres d'hotes in the surrounding area.

> Follow the same route back to the canal.

Follow the path towards Agen. It joins a road for a few metres before it separates on the right. Pont de Chicot (PK 118.230) is 900m from Sérignac. Cross a road and continue through shade above the canal to Pont de Plaisance, 1.4km away. Cross the Ruisseau de Bagneauque with a very steep drop. Join a road for 300m and reach Pont de Colomay. The canal broadens before the bridge with a nice shady area for a rest. There is a sign for Sainte-Colombe-en-Bruilhois (5km). Continue on the path above the canal crossing La Seynes stream with a deep drop and immediately afterwards a canalet with a sluice gate. This links to the Garonne river to your

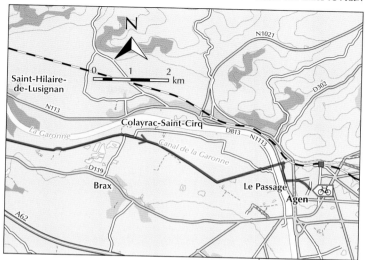

left. The Brax pumping station on the river supplements the canal's water supply. There is a sign for Brax (2km) at the next bridge, Pont Nodieier. Cross a road and continue on a road for 300m on the north bank and then rejoin the cycle track. The path joins a road again before Pont de Fresons (PK 111,255) and continues on another before reaching a bridge/lock, Écluse (37) de Rosette. You can see the next lock ahead of you while there are signs for Le Passage d'Agen and Roquefort Parc Walibi to the right.

The path becomes crowded as you approach Agen. Écluse (36) Chabieres is just 405m from the previous lock and 391m from the next, Marianette (35). Écluse d'Agen is a further 400m towards Agen and marks the beginning of the aqueduct over the Garonne river. The towpath is 2m wide on either side and it is recommended that you keep a foot on the ground when crossing.

The idea for an **aqueduct** was conceived by Jean-Baptiste de Baudre, while Monsieur Job was its

*The aqueduct at Agen*

engineer. It was modelled on similar river crossings on the Canal du Midi but was the first of its kind on the Garonne canal. The Duke of Orleans, eldest son of the presumptive king Louis Phillipe, laid the first stone on the 25 August 1839. The aqueduct was completed on the 22 October 1842. It is 580m in length and 12.5m in width with 23 arches each 20m wide spanning the river at a height of 10m. There are wonderful views of the Garonne and the town from it. The Château d'Eau (Pump House) is beneath the bridge.

There is a cycle track (1.3km) into the town which gives great views of the aqueduct from the Garonne riverbank. At the end of the aqueduct join a road on your left and turn left, going back in the direction you came. The road bends sharply to the left and you pass the Château d'Eau. Take a cycle track on the left marked Agen Centre Ville. Pass under the aqueduct and then over a small waterway, La Masse. There is an excellent viewing platform on your right 800m from the aqueduct. Climb the steps to get a good view. Continue until you reach a road. Turn left onto rue des Îles passing a playground on your left. Reach the main road (D813) and turn right and left at Place Jasmine. ◄

You can also reach the centre by leaving the aqueduct and climbing to the road bridge in front of you. Turn right and follow the main road (D813) towards the centre.

## AGEN

*The theatre in Place
Docteur Pierre Esquirol*

The medium-sized town of Agen, with a population of approximately 35,000, is famed for its prunes (*pruneaux* d'Agen) but it has a lot more to offer than dried plums. The aqueduct carrying the canal is the prime attraction for cyclists but other sights are worth visiting.

Relatively modern with wide well-planned avenues and an old town at its heart, Agen is important as the midway point between Bordeaux and Toulouse and as a marketplace for fruit and vegetables produced in the region. It is a transport hub too as it is close to the A62 motorway and has a railway station making it easy to reach for cyclists and others. Culturally, Agen has a municipal theatre and art gallery. SU-Agen is a well-known professional rugby team based in the town.

The town benefitted from the opening of the Canal du Midi in the 17th century as boats brought goods from Bordeaux and Toulouse along the Garonne river to or from the canal's beginning in Toulouse. The famous Agen prunes were sold to sailors and other travellers going to Bordeaux to sail for the New World. They ate these to avoid scurvy. The town also profited from the trade with the New World, growing wealthy in tandem with Bordeaux. Agen has been home to several famous people including Nostradamus who settled in the town to practise medicine in 1531. Another, Matteo Bandello, was an Italian clergyman and author who was forced to flee Milan after the fall of Lombardy in 1525. William Shakespeare based some of his plays, such as *Romeo and Juliet*, on Bandello's stories. The poet Jacques Boé, also known as Jasmin, was born in the town in 1798. He published in both

French and Occitan. His writing was recognised by the Académie Française, the academy of Toulouse and Pope Pious IX.

Two boulevards give you access to the town. Boulevard de la République (D813) as mentioned and Boulevard President Carnot which leaves Place Rebelais from the railway station.

Two squares are well worth visiting: Place des Laitiers (Square of the Dairy) and Place Docteur Pierre Esquirol. The former is at the centre of the old town and was a medieval trading hub. It has arcades on three sides with cafés and shops under these. The tourist office is beside this square.

Three important buildings face onto Place Docteur Pierre Esquirol: the town hall, the Ducourneau Theatre and the Musée des Beaux-Arts. The museum's main attraction is a set of five paintings by Goya including a self-portrait. Many of Agen's half-timbered houses are found on the 15th-century rue Beauville, close to the square.

The Cathédral St-Caprais is the town's most important church. It faces Place du Maréchal Foch. It dates from the 12th century but it has been much changed since that time. It was restored as a church in 1796 and elevated to the status of cathedral in 1801. It is cruciform and has frescoes showing the martyrdom of Agen saints, as well as the Evangelists and the Apostles.

Externally, there are carvings of monsters, animals and people.

The Église des Jacobins (the Church of the Jacobins) dates from the 13th century. The Dominicans, known as the Jacobins, established their monastery in Agen in 1249. The main church is all that remains. Built of red brick, it has two high naves. Some of the original wall decorations remain with geometrical shapes creating optical illusions. The church

*The beautiful interior of Église des Jacobins*

is now used as an exhibition space and there is a charge for entry. It is well worth a visit.

The church of Sainte-Foy is dedicated to a virgin martyr of the same name. It is at the end of Boulevard President Carnot and opposite the railway station.

The Walibi-Aquitane is an amusement park approximately 4km from Agen. Cyclists will have seen a sign for this near the start of Agen's aqueduct. It is situated southwest of the town and offers river rafting, amusement rides, sound and light and sea lion shows.

Agen is a good place to stop on the canal with plenty of hotels suited to most budgets plus lots of restaurants, cafés, bars and food outlets in the town and, throughout summer, it is alive with festivals and concerts.

*Ste-Foy church across the road from the railway station*

## EXCURSION 1
*To Port-Sainte-Marie and Clermont-Dessous*

| | |
|---|---|
| **Start** | Pont de Thomas (PK 127,580) |
| **Distance** | 20km |
| **Accumulated climb** | 91m |
| **Path** | Asphalt road |
| **Map** | IGN TOP100 160 |
| **Detour** | Point Fenêtre d'Observation |

This short excursion takes small roads through the Garonne plain passing orchards and fields of arable crops. It brings you across the Garonne to the medieval port of Port-Sainte-Marie with its old half-timbered houses and narrow streets. You then climb to the medieval village of Clermont-Dessous whose church is visible for several kilometres from the towpath. A further climb brings you to a viewing point with panoramas of the Garonne and Masse valleys. The route returns through pleasant countryside passing the Moulin St Laurent before rejoining the canal.

Leave the canal bridge, Pont de Thomas (PK 127,580). Cross to the north side of the canal and continue on this road. Pass a small lake/reservoir on your left. You can see Clermont-Dessous church on the hill to your right. At the top of the lake turn left and quickly reach apple and kiwi orchards. Cross over a canalette, les Coulets, and 3km from the canal reach a crossroads with five roads leading into it. Turn right and in 800m reach a junction with a slightly larger road. Turn right (you can see a main road to your left). There is a small waterfall on your right obscured by some trees. Cycle alongside this small river before crossing it by bridge to reach a crossroads, car-refour de la Bacôte. Turn left onto rue de Prieuré, 4.5km from the canal. The ancient priory from which the road is named is on your left and not in great repair; the building on the right is in an even worse state.

Turn right onto a small road with a view of Clermont-Dessous church ahead. This brings you to **Saint-Laurent** with memorials left and right. The village has some businesses and a tabac/café. It was once a centre for rope-making supplying boats plying the river Garonne. Turn left onto the main road (D213) with some shaded park space between you and the river. Veer right and cross the Garonne bridge. This gives a good view of Port-Sainte-Marie. ▶ Descend to a roundabout on the town side. Take a small road on your right and follow this under the railway track. Turn right immediately on to a small road with a worn cycle track. Watch for rue de Prieuré on your left. Turn here to reach Place les Templiers. You are in the old centre of **Port-Sainte-Marie**, just over 7km from the canal.

*Port-Sainte-Marie viewed from the Garonne bridge*

What looks like the confluence of two rivers upriver (to your right as you face Port Sainte-Marie) is in fact two branches of the Garonne.

## PORT-SAINTE-MARIE

Port-Sainte-Marie traces its origins to the Romans. Its site was attractive for those navigating the river and it developed into a prosperous port from the 12th century. onwards. Although the town is now rundown and shabby it is still well worth a visit. There are plenty of half-timbered houses on its narrow streets and it has small shops and a café in its centre, while there is a restaurant on its outskirts. There is a train station on the Bordeaux to Toulouse line

*Figurines in an alcove above the street*

with trains every hour to two hours in both directions.

The Knights Templars built a church in Place les Templiers in the 12th century. The square is dilapidated but interesting, especially the small dancing figurines in an alcove above a door. The parish church of Notre Dame was founded in the 11th or 12th century and the present church dates in part from the 14th century (but was still under construction 100 years later). The interior is worth a look with a stellar sky design in the copula.

Catherine de Medici stayed here, and during her stay her daughter Margot came to visit her. There is a monument, Les Trois Fontaines (The Three Fountains), which is said to mark the spot where Margot met the future king, Henry IV. This is on rue Dr Chanteloube set down from the road so you need to keep your eyes peeled to spot it.

Continuing to Clermont-Dessous, leave Place les Templiers in the direction of the river Garonne and turn left. Use the cycle lane and rise to a junction. The church of Notre Dame is on your left. Turn right following a sign for Agen onto rue Pasteur which becomes the D118E. You cross a small river, La Masse, which lends its name to the valley it flows through. Pass through the hamlet of Tivoli, 2km from Port-Sainte-Marie. Leave the D118E turning left following a sign for Clermont-Dessous on the D245C and climb up this road as it goes through a number of hairpins

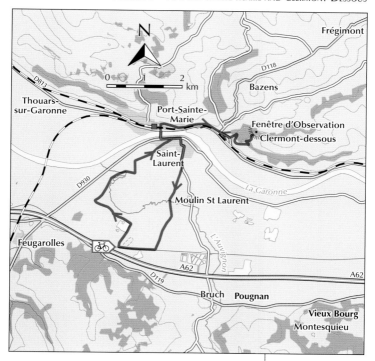

for 1km coming to a turn to the left that leads to the medieval village of **Clermont-Dessous**.

**Clermont-Dessous**, perched on a narrow outcrop overlooking the Garonne, its valley to the south and the Masse valley to the north, is a lovely village with narrow streets, old stone houses, a church and a ruined castle. The village was fortified in medieval times and the church, Église Jean Bapiste, is an excellent example of Romanesque architecture. It dates from the 12th century and later became a priory for the Benedictines attached to the monastery at Clairac. It is in a cruciform shape with a bare

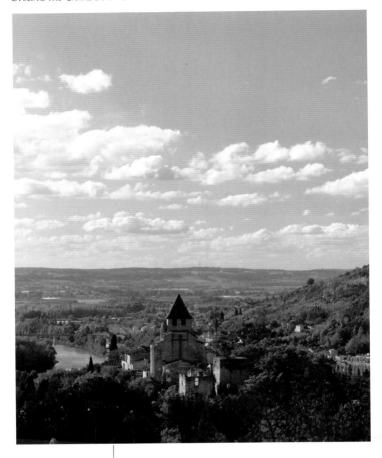

*Clermont-Dessous and the Garonne from the viewpoint*

stone interior and tall pillars rising up to and supporting the cupola.

The castle tower dates from the 13th century; it was built to protect the village on its most exposed side. The castle itself is owned privately and is being restored gradually.

There is a viewpoint above the village which gives an excellent panorama over the river and surrounding countryside. Continue on the same road you reached the village. It bends to the right and follow signs for Point Fenêtre d'Observation which you reach in 600m (124m elevation). This gives a view of the confluence of the two valleys – the Garonne and the Masse. You have a wonderful view along the river and back towards Clermont-Dessous's double-belled church spire with the river behind it. To your right as you face the village is the Masse Valley.

Return to Port-Sainte-Marie by the same route but follow the one-way system cycling through the town on the road, rue Dr Chanteloube, with Notre Dame church immediately on your right. Turn left at a stop sign at the end of the road onto rue Jules Guesde and pass under a railway bridge following a sign for Lavardac. Then pass under a road bridge. Turn left onto a very busy road and almost immediately turn left again and climb up to the road bridge you just passed under. Cross the bridge over the Garonne on the D930. Turn left at the end of the bridge onto the D213 and cycle through Saint-Laurent.

There is a different route back to the canal from here. Continue on the road to a stop sign where you turn right following a sign for Bruch (among other places). The road bends left and right and 1km from the junction take a small road to the right immediately after a large farmstead (also on the right) with small signposts for Bécane, Hauret and Le Moulin. Pass a number of large farmhouses and yards. You will see a large redbrick chimney with a large house and buildings beside it. This is the Moulin St Laurent which offers farm camping, gîtes and chambres d'hôtes. Cross a bridge over the mill race. Continue to a bridge over the canal which you cross and double-back slightly to regain the canal path on the south bank at Pont de St Martin (PK 126,600). ▶

If you wish to return to the starting point, Pont de Thomas, just short of a kilometre away, turn right towards Bordeaux.

117

## EXCURSION 2
*To Nérac*

| | |
|---|---|
| **Start** | Écluse (38) l'Auvignon |
| **Distance** | 28.4km |
| **Accumulated climb** | 448m |
| **Path** | Asphalt road |
| **Map** | IGN TOP100 160 |
| **Detour** | Espiens |

This excursion takes you on quiet roads and through hills to the medieval town of Nérac on the river Bäise. It passes through Bruch and climbs to Espiens. The round trip is almost 30km and includes an accumulated climb of 448m. It follows the D136 which is a relatively quiet road. There are no shops between Bruch and Nérac.

The town is described in Stage 4 as a detour.

Leave the canal at Écluse (38) l'Auvignon: there are signs for Bruch (1.5km) and Nérac (12km). Follow these as you head south paying attention to the traffic lights on the bridge. Take a bridge over a motorway (**A62**) and then cross a junction with the **D199**. Follow a sign for **Bruch** centre. Come to a second stop sign, cross the road and take a left turn. Note the gate tower and old Bruch on the left. ◄

Turn right almost immediately following a sign for Nérac. The road climbs and swings right. Pass the church with Jardin de l'Abbé Lacaze in front of it. Stay on the D136 as it climbs and bends. Pass a turn to the left for Calignac and head towards a clump of trees. The road continues through arable land with little shade and few houses. There are good views of the countryside to your left. Reach a sign for Château de Mazelières (5.7km from canal), a 17th-century chateau with an elegant square courtyard offering expensive accommodation. There is a very modern wine producer on your

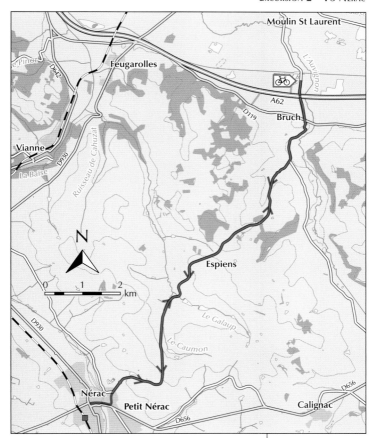

right with large metallic-silver vats beside it. This produces a Buzet wine.

You will see a church spire to your left as you climb.
Reach a junction with a sign indicating left for **Espiens**.

The village of **Espiens** is 450m from the road; the
junction is 7km from where you left the canal

and has an elevation of 131m, while the village is 193m. Notre Dame church is its main building and there is a good panorama of the surrounding countryside towards the canal and Garonne. The quiet village does not have a shop or any other services.

The D136 climbs through open arable countryside towards a water tower. You reach the road that leads to the water tower 11.3km from the canal (elevation 171m). Descend rapidly, passing a Nérac town sign. Go straight through the roundabout, following signs for Nérac. Turn left at the next roundabout (church ahead on your left) using a cycle track on your right. Follow this as it swings right alongside a busy main road (D656). There is an entrance into a park, Parc Royal de la Garenne. The chateau is ahead and below it is the Pont Neuf. Cross this and the square on your right heralds your arrival to the centre of **Nérac**, just over 14km from the canal.

*The chateau in Nérac*

## NÉRAC

*Nérac harbour on the river Baïse*

Nérac is a medieval town on the river Bäise. It is famed as the former home of Henry IV, known as good king Henry. Only part of Henry's chateau remains and it houses a museum. This wing is one of the original four and gives a sense of the majesty of the entire structure. The museum recalls the region's history and has artefacts associated with the Albret family.

Nérac was the capital of medieval Albret and the power centre for the House of Albret. The town has excellent examples of 15th- and 16th-century houses including those on the docks of the river Bäise whose loggia overlook the river. Rue Séderie on the other bank to the chateau is parallel to the river and has half-timbered houses on both sides. This leads to the old bridge, le Pont Vieux. Maison de Sully at the corner of rue Séderie and rue de Sully dates from the latter part of the 16th century.

The Pont Vieux is humpbacked and links the two medieval banks of the town. There is a good view of what were tannery houses on the right as you look upstream towards the Pont Neuf. There are craft shops and some art galleries in these now.

The Church of Saint-Nicolas is the town's main church replacing an earlier 10th-century one which had fallen into disrepair. The interior murals were added in the 19th century and were painted by Gustave Lasalle-Bordes.

They depict sin and temptation and address the danger of succumbing to the temptation of Protestantism.

The Parc Royal de la Garenne was developed on the site of a Roman villa. It was created in the 16th century by Jeanne d'Albret and Antoine de Bourbon, father of Henry IV, and expanded by Queen Margot, Henry's first wife. The walk is shaded by oak and elms, some dating back centuries. One of the more curious items in the park is a statue of a young woman, Fleurette. The legend has it that young Henry broke her heart and grief drove her to drown herself in the river. The King's bathing house may be reached by footbridge. The park has a pavilion, tennis courts, picnic spots and open spaces.

*A typical half-timbered house in Nérac*

Follow the same route to return to the canal. Leave from the Pont Neuf and follow the D656 remembering to swing left onto the D136 as you leave the town. Take the first exit to the right at the first roundabout and go straight through the second. The ascent from Nérac is steep but once you reach the water tower it is an easy descent to the canal with good views over the Garonne plain.

## STAGE 5
*Agen to Moissac*

| | |
|---|---|
| **Start** | Pont Saint Georges |
| **Distance** | 45km |
| **Accumulated climb** | 55m |
| **Path** | Asphalt cycle track and road |
| **Map** | IGN TOP100 160 and 161 |
| **Detours** | Castelculier and Villascopia (3km); Valence d'Agen (1.2km); St Nicolas de la Grave (7km) |
| **Excursion** | Auvillar (10.5km) |

Some beautiful villages and towns are passed through on this lovely stage, which also includes a number of detours and a short excursion to Auvillar, described as one of the most beautiful villages in France. The first detour is to the Roman remains at Castelculier where there is an interesting audio-visual display of Roman life. The route passes close to the Golfech nuclear facility before reaching the point of the next detour, to the important town of Valence d'Agen. The last detour takes in St Nicolas de la Grave, the location of one of Richard the Lionheart's chateaus. Finally Moissac is reached, at the confluence of the Garonne and Tarn rivers, a town with one of the oldest intact monastic cloisters in Europe.

Follow the D813 north to the bridge, Pont Saint Georges, over the canal. Descend to the slightly shaded path on the north bank and take the asphalt rather than the grit path. You are asked to walk your bike under the next bridge, 100m further on. Follow the path for 1.2km to a harbour with picnic tables. Dismount again to pass under the next bridge after which there is a marked cycle track.

Go under another bridge (2.2km from Agen) with a school to your left. Pass a spillover and go under two more bridges. The road veers to the left before a metal bridge while you stay on the cycle path. The path rises slightly as you pass a slipway and dips under a bridge. The canal widens briefly at this point. Pass a long parklike

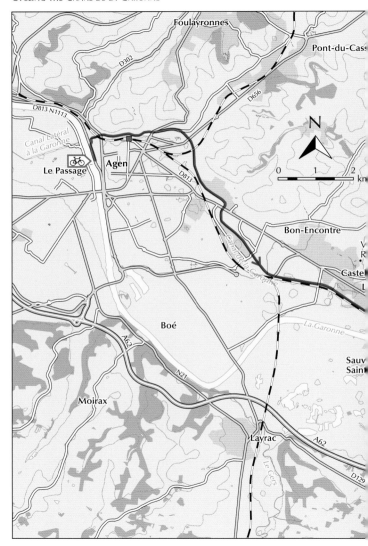

strip and reach Pont du Pourret (PK 101.975) (6.5km from Agen). There are two bridges together. Reach Boé Port. This has taps, toilets, a playground and a tourist office. It is a good location for a picnic but there are no shops. Shortly afterwards, pass a spillover and note a beautiful turreted chateau on your left, the 17th-century Château Saint Marcel Hotel. Pass under a new bridge and come to Pont de St Marcel. Reach Pont de Les Carbonnères (8.7km from Agen) and climb to the road. There are cycle signs for Villascopia (villa Gallo Romaines), Castelculier 0.5km and St Pierre de Gaubert 2km.

**Detour to Castelculier and Villascopia**
Take the road north at Pont de Les Carbonnères, Route du Canal, D443. The bridge crossing is regulated by traffic lights and although you do not cross the bridge you

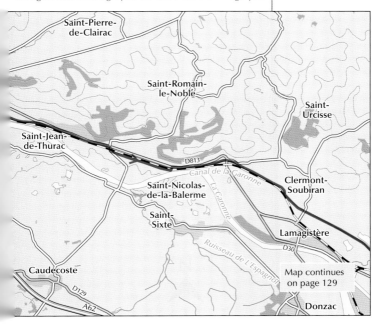

Map continues on page 129

should be wary of traffic coming through quickly on green. In 400m reach a roundabout. There is a hotel, the Akena City Agen, on the left. Take the second exit. Be careful as you have to cross a very busy road, the D813. Follow Avenue Jean Monnet passing the shops and services at **Castelculier** and come to a small roundabout – note a small *lavoir* ahead of you. Take the left turn onto Rue de Lamarque and follow this to the **Villascopia**.

The remains of a fourth-century **Roman villa** are the chief attraction in the small town of Castelculier, north of the canal. These include fully excavated thermal baths making it one of the most important examples of its kind in the Aquitaine. The Villascopia, across the road from the villa's ruins, has an exhibition of artefacts found in the excavations. There is also a 3D film, the scénovision, which shows what life was like here in fourth century. There are guided tours or you can visit the excavations on your own.

Return to the canal by the same route.

*The remains of the Roman villa in Castelculier*

Descend to the canal on the north side after crossing the road. The railway track to Toulouse is close to the canal on the other bank. The path shares a road for 400m. Come to a tall aqueduct over the river Séoune, a Garonne tributary, which flows close to Castelculier. You will see steam clouds rising from the two cooling towers of the nuclear power plant at Golfech. Cycle past the entrance to some works on your left, yielding to traffic if necessary, and climb to the Pont d'Ostande which is 1km from Pont de Les Carbonnères. Pass a park on you left and enter **Lafox**.

> **Lafox** has a castle which dates from the 12th century. It controlled a ford over the river Séoune. Le Manoir de Prades dates from the 17th century and was the birthplace of the poet Cortes de Prades (1586-1667), one of the most cultured minds in the court of Louis XIII. He composed in the Agenais dialect.

The path follows the road and veers slightly from the canal. Take a sharp right to rejoin it. Pass a pond behind some trees and climb to the road at Pont de Sauveterre (97.6km).

Cross the road and pass a church on the hill above the canal. This is the Church of St Christopher and is popular for weddings. Come to the bridge/lock, Écluse de Saint Christophe (33), 12.6km from Agen and 3.1km from the next lock le Noble. ▶

The lock keeper's house is a B&B, Auberge de la Poule à Vélo (the Hen with a Bike), with a restaurant and café and a lovely wisteria above the door.

Continue on a quiet path with little shade, passing under the Pont de Carrere, and reach **Saint-Jean-de-Thurac** on your left as you cycle beside a busy road (D813). Cross a road at Pont de Guillemis yielding to traffic. In a little over a kilometre reach a shaded picnic/meeting area. There is a monument to those who died fighting for France from the region. Climb to the bridge/lock, Écluse de Noble (32) and cross the canal to the southside. ▶ In 1.5km join a road and shortly afterwards come to a bridge where you cross to the north bank. ▶ There are views of the Garonne river to your

Change to the south bank.

Change to the north bank.

*La Poule à Vélo*

right as well as of the Golfech cooling towers ahead. You are requested to slow down and stay on the right as you pass under the next bridge. There are signs for Clermont-Soubiran (3km) and Puymirol (8km) to the north. There are also kilometre signs for the main towns along the path with the final destination, Toulouse, being 91km away. In under 2km, climb to Pont Saint Pierre (PK 88,450) and note a view of a church and chateau on the hill. Cross the bridge and rejoin the path on the southside. ◄ There are no signs here to indicate this change. You pass under another bridge before coming to the next bridge/lock, Écluse (31) Lamagistère which is 6.9km from the previous lock, Noble, and 6.3km from the next at Valence d'Agen. **Lamagistère** has a bakery, convenience store, hotel and railway station served only by local trains.

Change to the
south bank.

Pass under the next bridge named after the river Barguelonne which you cross over shortly afterwards on an aqueduct. The iron railings are worth a closer look. The Barguelonne is a Garonne tributary. The village of **Golfech** is to the south as you reach the bridge named after it where there is a convenience store and a restaurant.

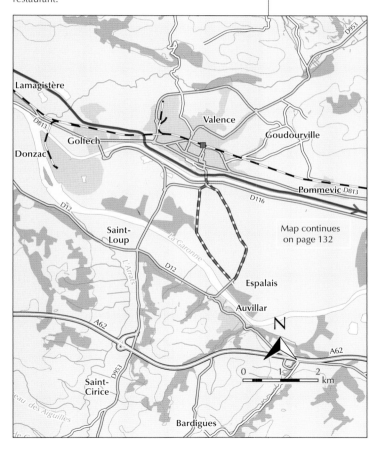

Map continues on page 132

129

There are two pressurised water reactors in the **Golfech nuclear complex** on an island formed by the Garonne and the Golfech canal; the canal provides the cooling water for the reactors. The plant employs over 900 people and its cooling towers are the tallest in Europe.

Pass under three bridges: Golfech, Coupet and a railway bridge. The Golfech canal is on your right. The next bridge, Roux, has nice red brickwork. A tall church steeple and a red-bricked chimney mark your approach to Valence-d'Agen: you arrive at Valence d'Agen bridge 3km from Golfech's bridge.

### Detour to Valence d'Agen
To reach the town from the canal path, climb to Valence d'Agen bridge. You pass a parking place for camper vans as you do. Cross the bridge and Valence port is on your right.

There is a gradual climb to the town. Climb a steeper road into the town centre and follow the main road eastwards into Place National.

**Valence d'Agen**, founded by King Edward I of England in 1283 and a good example of an English *bastide*, is famed for its three *lavoirs* and a dovecote. You passed the circular Lavoir del Théron, a red-tiled building on the right, as you climbed into town. This was built towards the end of the 18th century, and a spring provided the water. The town has two market places, one a metallic construction, and the other, an older, covered market in the Place National. The town has several attractive sculptures and fountains close to the main square and the church is at its edge. The architecture is typical of the region and it is well worth wandering the town's streets. To see the dovecote take the road towards Cahors to the outskirts of the town in the Place du Columbier.

There is a large open space behind the port where the annual **Au Fil de l'Eau** (Across the

Water) spectacle is staged in early August. Some 350 people take part portraying canal life since its inception.

The town has a hotel, chambre d'hote, and there is a campsite on its outskirts near the stadium and tennis club. There are a number of restaurants, shops and services.

Return to the canal path by the same route or alternatively by the D11 to Pont Auvillar.

From the south side of Valence d'Agen bridge, follow the path for 600m to Auvillar bridge. ▶ Opposite the next lock reached, Écluse (30) Valence, is Château de Lantourne, a nice chateau with an ironwork folly.

Auvillar bridge is the starting point for the excursion to Auvillar village: see below.

131

Reach Gauge bridge (PK 79,074) and then Écluse (29) Pommevic. **Pommevic** port and village are on the opposite bank. The village has a shop and bakery. Leave at Pont de Pommevic to visit the village.

Écluse (28) du Braguel is 700m from Pommevic bridge. The central nuclear canal is on the other side of an embankment on your right. The canal widens at an industrial works opening onto the canal. Approach **Malause** and reach Pont Palor 2km from Braguel lock. ◄ The *halte nautique* in Malause, on the opposite bank, commemorates Georges Stehlin who died fighting for France in Morocco in 1955 aged 23. Join a road after the bridge,

Take this bridge if you wish to visit the town, 400m off route.

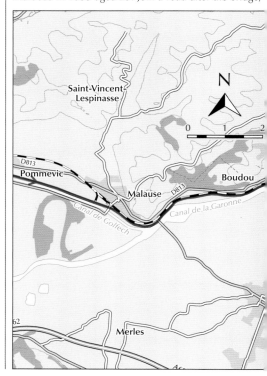

come to Pont de Malause and pass under its arches. The river is close by. Reach the bridge/lock of Petit Bezy (27) and then, 2km further on, come to a blue iron suspension bridge.

### Detour to Saint-Nicolas-de-la-Grave

Steps lead up to the suspension bridge and there is a sign for Saint-Nicolas-de-la-Grave at their base. Guttering beside the steps allows you to wheel your bike up but with difficulty as the steps are steep. ▶ Cross the suspension bridge, Pont de Coudal (PK 69,240); with only one traffic lane, caution is advised. Follow the road, **D15**,

It is advisable to remove panniers etc and carry these separately.

133

towards Saint-Nicolas passing the Base de Loisirs on your left.

> **Base de Loisirs** is a centre for watersports, camping and outdoor activities. It is on the shore of a lake formed by the confluence of the Garonne and Tarn rivers. There is an island known as the Bird Island, Île aux Oiseaux, which is a sanctuary and a stopping point for migrating birds.

The village comes into view about 2.5km from the bridge and you reach **Saint-Nicolas-de-la-Grave** on a road that leads directly to a church.

> **Saint-Nicolas-de-la-Grave** dates from Roman times. It was founded by the monastery in Moissac and its charter dates from 1135 as one of the 'sauvetés'. These were refuges around a church where people found asylum.
>
> The chateau is the village's most significant monument. It is a large, square red-bricked building with four towers on its corners. It dates from the 12th century but it was probably built on the site of an earlier building. The Garonne flowed close to the chateau in medieval times. Richard the Lionheart lived there at the end of the 12th century. It now houses local municipal services. One of the village's quirkier attractions is the Musée Lamothe-Cadillac (Cadillac Museum). This commemorates Antoine Laumet de la Mothe, sieur de (Sir) Cadillac known as Antoine de la Mothe-Cadillac, who was born in the house that is now the museum. He founded Detroit in 1701 and was subsequently governor of Louisiana. A larger than life character, he engaged in fur-trading and alcohol smuggling among other things. He was held in such high regard in Detroit that it was decided to name the Cadillac car, produced in Detroit, in his honour. The village has three churches, the largest of which is in the arcaded main square.

Return to the canal by the same route on the D15.

*The red-bricked Napoleon bridge*

Continue for almost 2km and climb to the bridge/lock Écluse (26) l'Espagnette. There is a chateau in the distance on the other bank. Cross a stream, the Madeleine. The track is now beside the Tarn river. Shortly after, you see Napoleon bridge over the Tarn at Moissac.

Pass Moissac sewage works as you enter the town and shortly after join a road. Follow this to a roundabout at a bridge. It is not possible to continue beside the canal as the canal-side road is one-way in the opposite direction. Take a road to the right. Descend towards the river passing a primary school (Ecole de Montebello) on your right. Join a cycle path on your right to go under the Napoleon bridge. There are two options after the bridge: either stay beside the river and pass between it and the Hotel Moulin de Moissac (Moissac mill) or more simply join the road and pass in front of the hotel. Come to a roundabout. Take the first exit and pass an art deco restaurant and bar on your right. Climb up the road in front of you and come to the canal, Descente en Tarn, a short channel linking the Garonne canal with the Tarn river.

## MOISSAC

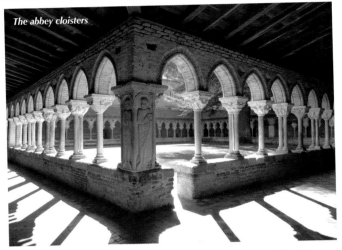
The abbey cloisters

Moissac is home to what was an important monastery in medieval times. It is also a major centre for fruit production and the local Chasselas grape was the first fruit to be awarded an AOC. The canal goes through the town centre and it is worth exploring its length. One interesting feature is the Saint-Jacques Bridge which swings to one side allowing boats to pass through. Townsfolks have processions on the canal during festivals and national celebrations. The roads along the river are closed to all traffic and are jammed with people and fairground attractions during these festivities.

The Abbey of St-Pierre de Moissac was founded in the seventh century. It grew in importance to become one of the most significant in the southwest of France. It is a UNESCO heritage site and a centre for pilgrims on the Camino de Santiago de Compostela. The abbey's main attraction is its cloister built in the 11th century (there is a charge for entry). It is the oldest example of an intact cloisters in Europe. Its four galleries have a total of 76 marble columns.

The monastery developed a scriptorium (a library where books were copied) which was renowned throughout Western Europe receiving visitors from other, far-flung centres of learning. There is an exhibition about this in the cloisters. It is well worth climbing by a back-stairs to the church tower. A room at the top of this looks down into the church itself. There is also a model of a 10th-century organ reconstructed from plans and images. The church's southern door is topped by a spectacular tympanum – the semi-circular arch over the door – representing Christ in his majesty. Within the church are carved sculptures.

Moissac is a market town and the main square, Place des Récollets, is home to the open market, the municipal and fish markets. These bustle during market days. Stalls sell everything from food to bric-à-brac.

The Tarn riverbank is also well worth exploring. The impressive main bridge, Pont Napoléon spanning the Tarn, is built of red stone and was completed in 1825. It has nine arches and is 187m long.

The town has two classic hotels: the Pont Napoléon and the Moulin de Moissac. The former is beside Napoleon's bridge while the latter is upriver towards the junction with the canal. Both have restaurants. Moulin de Moissac was formerly a water-powered mill.

Le Kiosque d'Ulvarium is one of Moissac's jewels. It is an art deco kiosk which is both a bar and restaurant. The interior decoration is worth the price of a drink to view. The exterior too is striking and it is a good place to relax and watch the sun set near Napoleon's bridge after a warm day's cycling.

### EXCURSION 3
*To Auvillar*

| | |
|---|---|
| **Start** | Pont Auvillar |
| **Distance** | 10.5km |
| **Accumulated climb** | 60m |
| **Path** | Small roads |
| **Map** | IGN TOP100 160 |

Auvillar is described as one of the most beautiful villages in France. Perched on a rocky outcrop, it has wonderful views of the Garonne river, its plain and the village's old port. Its many attractions include its circular covered grain market and its wonderful clocktower and gate. It attracts pilgrims en route to Santiago de Compostela and artists painting the stunning views and picturesque buildings. It also has a reputation for producing pottery and goose-feather quills. The short excursion takes minor roads to Auvillar and returns on the larger busier road (D11). Those wishing to avoid this road can return via the outward route.

Leave the canal path at Pont Auvillar where there is cycle signpost for Auvillar (6km). Climb to the main road. Cross a larger bridge using the cycle track heading south and over both the canal and the canal de la centrale nucléaire. Come to a roundabout and follow the inner cycle path taking the first exit to the right. Cross a small road off to the right and immediately take a left turn at a small roundabout following signs for camping, the stadium and an equestrian school. Pass the municipal camping, right, and the stadium, left. Turn left at a junction with a slightly larger road, 1.7km from the canal, with a sign for Espalais. Pass planted woodland, right, and later a golf course, left. In 2km you arrive at a roundabout and will see the village of **Espalais** in front. Turn right onto the D11 following a sign for Auvillar (2km). Cross a suspension bridge over the Garonne river and stay on the road noting

a turn to the left for Auvillar port. The main road climbs steeply passing a kilometre sign. There are good views of the Garonne and surrounding countryside to your left. Enter **Auvillar** through the 18th-century clocktower gate on the left and onto Rue de l'Horloge.

*Auvillar is a pilgrimage site*

Rue de l'Horloge takes you to **Place de la Halle** where you will find the circular grain market built of red brick. It dates from the 19th century when it replaced the older traditional square market. The houses around the square, actually triangular in shape, are arcaded. There are attractive houses on the streets leading off from the square. Go past the tourist office to reach a viewing terrace with spectacular views over the Garonne and the plain. The rest of the village is also well worth exploring. St Peter's church was originally a Benedictine Abbey dating from the 12th century.

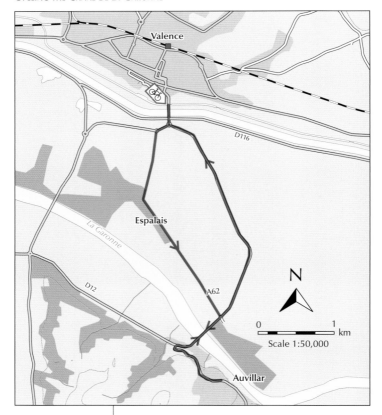

Leave the village by the same road that you entered it. Cross the bridge and come to the roundabout. Continue straight on to return to Valence by the D11. You pass the Château de Lastours (chambre d'hôte) on your left and some of its buildings on your right. Stay on the road until you reach a roundabout which was the first one you encountered on the outward leg. Take the right turn and cross the bridge to rejoin the canal path on the other side.

Auvillar's 18th-century clocktower gate

## STAGE 6
*Moissac to Montauban*

| | |
|---|---|
| **Start** | Descente dans le Tarn locks |
| **Distance** | 37km |
| **Accumulated climb** | 75m |
| **Path** | Asphalt cycle track and small roads |
| **Map** | IGN TOP100 161 |

This stage links two major towns on the canal system. The latter part follows the canal extension which joins Montech to Montauban. Leaving Moissac, the canal crosses the Tarn river by way of a 356m-long aqueduct. This is not the only interesting engineering feature: there is a water slope, a mechanical device for lifting barges past a series of locks, on the approach to Montech. You come close to some of the canal's industrial heritage in Montech port before following the canal extension to Montauban. This links the canal back to the river Tarn. Montauban is the pink-bricked capital of the Tarn et Garonne region and one of the most attractive towns in the area. Its central square, Place Nationale, is stunning.

Stay on the south bank.

A Montauban man, Pierre Gausserand, oversaw its construction.

At the double lock, Descente dans le Tarn, cross from the town to the opposite bank. This short canal links the Garonne canal to the Tarn river. The path swings right to the Écluse (25) Moissac with a footbridge. ◄ The next lock is 600m further on: Écluse (24) Gregonne; Écluse (23) du Cacor is approximately the same distance further on. The 13-arched aqueduct crossing the Tarn is ahead, 2km from the centre. ◄ The path surface is cobbled and you can see a metal railway bridge in the distance upriver.

Continue on a picturesque well-shaded straight path. A sign for Hotel/Restaurant Felix to the right at Pont Caussade (PK 60,531) alerts you to the Wild West themed hotel. Pass under the bridge. Écluse (22) d'Artel is 4km from Moissac. The next two locks come in rapid

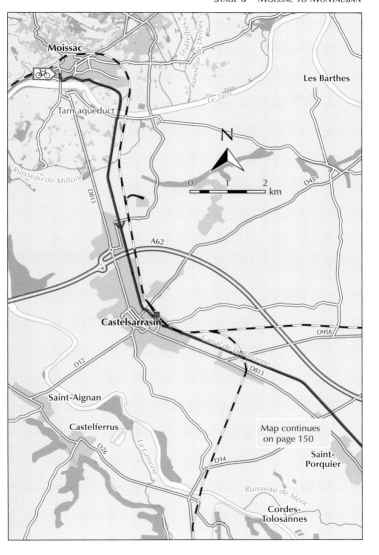

Map continues
on page 150

143

succession. There is a rare, minor discrepancy of 15m in the distances given on the lock houses between Artel and the next lock Écluse (21) Verries 470m away. Pass under a road bridge (D118) and come to the next lock, Écluse (20) de St Jean des Vignes in Castelsarrasin's outskirts. Pass under the next bridge and note a cycle track to the right leading to a commercial centre with a supermarket.

Reach Pont de l'Autoroute (PK 58,235) carrying the **A62** motorway, 6.4km from Moissac. Cross a small bridge over a bypass channel and climb to Écluse (19) Castelsarrasin. Cross the second small bridge over the bypass channel and pass under Pont de Gandalou and Pont de Castelsarrasin carrying the RD45. Reach Jaques-Yves Cousteau port in **Castelsarrasin** which has facilities including a Wi-Fi hotspot and a tourist office; its defining feature is a metal sculpture of a ship with birds flying over it surrounded by fountains. ◄

Follow the road south from the bridge to reach the centre of Castelsarrasin and its main square, Place des Belges.

## CASTELSARRASIN

The origin of the present-day name remains a mystery. The most recent and possibly the most likely explanation is that the name is derived from that of Raymond Sarraceni (also written Sarrasi), high dignitary of the Count of Toulouse in the 12th century responsible for building new towns in the region.

Saint Sauveur's church, 350m from Place des Belges, is first mentioned in AD961. Follow rue Edouard Herriot, turn left on to rue d'Égalité and then right onto rue de la République and continue straight to Place de la Raison where the church is on the right. It was assigned to the Moissac Abbey. The church has undergone extensive restoration and reconstruction over the centuries and suffered periods of neglect and decline. Some of the choir stalls were rescued by locals during the Revolution when much of the church's furniture was sold. These have been reinstated together with 12 other stalls which were donated. The elaborately carved pulpit is made, in part, from panels bought from the Abbey of Belleperche, 6km southeast of the town. The organ came from the same abbey and is listed as an historic monument.

Castelsarrasin has the usual shops, restaurants and a hotel in the centre. There is another hotel 2km from the town off the busy D813 in the Moissac direction. There are supermarkets in the suburbs, reached using the cycle track after St Jean des Vignes lock passed before reaching the town.

Port Jacques-Yves-Cousteau

Continue on the path noting a pedestrian bridge over the canal. The cycle path is marked in green on the left. Cross to the north bank at Pont de la Brunette (PK 56,00), using a cycle track separated from the road by kerbing stones. ▶ It drops to the left and turns a sharp left to pass under the bridge. The path runs beside a road.

Change to the north bank.

Reach Écluse (18) Prades 9.5km from Moissac. There is an old-style windmill on the opposite side of the canal about 400m further along the path. The next bridge (Cailhau) carries the D958, pass under it and shortly afterwards under a railway bridge. The spire to the right as you approach the next bridge belongs to the church in St Martin Belcassé. Dantous bridge is next, climb to it and cross the road. There is a chambre d'hôte a few hundred metres away from the canal on the left. The next bridge/lock is Pont Écluse (17) Saint-Martin (PK 51,920). Cross the road and after this cross a stream, the Ruisseau de Brouzidou. There are signs for La Ville Dieu du Temple (4km) and the Abbaye de Bellepeche (5km) at the next road bridge (D14), the Pont de Saint Andre (PK 50,642). ▶

The Knights Templar founded La Ville Dieu du Temple in the 12th century; in the 14th century it passed to the Knights of Malta and they held it until the Revolution.

145

The next road bridge was being renovated when this section of the canal was researched. The surrounding countryside is flat with extensive fruit and vegetable production. Pont Saint Porquier is next with the village of **Saint Porquier** less than 1km south. There are picnic tables on the opposite bank at the next bridge. Pass under this continuing on the north bank noting an aqueduct over Sanguinenc stream. Reach Pont Écluse (16) Escatalens (PK 47,49), 17.5km from Moissac. The land is intensively farmed with large fields of cereals growing close by. The Pont d'Escatalens is next. There is a sign for the village of **Escatalens**, 1km to the south. Watch for the next, large modern bridge, Pont Drimm, as the canal splits in two shortly after this. Stay on the northern bank as the path veers left. ◄ It comes close to a road but is separated from it by a wooden barrier. The locks on the other canal branch are visible from the path. The path stops at a bridge, **Pente d'Eau** (PK 44,420).

Stay on the north bank.

*The Pente d'Eau, meaning water slope*

In front of you is the **Pente d'Eau** (water slope), a mechanism that lifts boats up or down the 13.3m slope avoiding five locks. It was built in 1974 when there was sufficient traffic to justify its construction. The canal branch leading to this is 443m long. The slope has a 3 per cent gradient and only lifts boats over 30m long. Smaller boats must use the locks. Two electric engines power the lift taking 20 minutes to complete the ascent or descent. It is not in use at present.

To continue, cross the bridge and climb to the path in front of you. ▶ Turn left and pass Écluse (13) Pelllaborie and continue to Pont Écluse (12) des Peyrets (PK 43,890) where you cross to the south/left bank. ▶ There is a large overflow at this lock. Two chimneys come into view, with a church spire to the right. Cross a small steep bridge over an outlet followed by another to reach Écluse (11) de Montech. A harbour serves the old factory whose chimneys you have already seen.

> The **factory** building dates from 1856. It was originally a flour mill and then a paper mill powered by water turbines on the canal. The paper mill prospered through the first half of the 20th century. It employed up to 300 people. Competition, exchange rate problems and the costs of transporting materials and finished products saw it close in 1968. There are efforts being made to preserve the buildings as part of the town's architectural and historic heritage.

Immediately after the lock (11) note the confluence of the channel serving the water slope with the main canal. The beginning of the canal de Montech linking the town with Montauban is part of this junction and across the water. You are now in the port of **Montech**, 22.4km from Moissac, a popular stopping place for boaters.

Turn right if you wish to see the locks missed: Pommiés (15) and Escudiés (14). You must walk on the path to these as cycling is forbidden.

Change to the south bank.

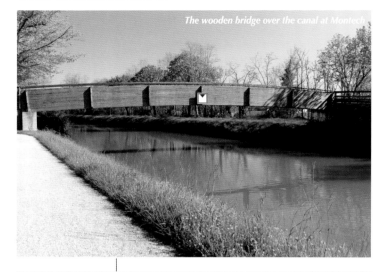
The wooden bridge over the canal at Montech

## MONTECH

Montech is a small port town developed on the *bastide* principle. Its main attraction is the Church of Our Lady of the Visitation. Built between 1358 and 1452, its steeple is close to 50m tall with a clarion of 17 bells.

Montech was a centre for the textile industry and there are several pink-bricked mansions reflecting the wealth generated. The town hall was originally a hospital and orphanage, Hôpital St-Esprit and the Larramet orphanage. There are also some half-timbered houses in the town.

The Café Bistrot Constant faces onto the canal at the port's edge. This is an architecturally re-imagined canal house with tables both inside and out. A playground and benches are close by. Pass under the bridge, Pont de Montech (PK 42,673) and reach a more extensive picnic area with toilets (hidden behind a hedge) and a water tap. This is a good place to stop for a picnic or longer break with shops, a campsite, hotel and all the usual facilities available in the centre.

Continue cycling on the south side and 600m from the café come to a wooden *passerelle* (foot/cycle bridge).

Cross this to the north bank. ▸

For Montauban, turn left, back in the direction you have been travelling, and follow the path on the north bank. ▸ Pass under the Pont de Montech again and veer right to pass under another bridge, Embouchement (mouth) du Canal de Montech (PK 0,060), carrying the D42, and join the Montech canal. The path is on the east bank for the entire length.

Pass a small lake, a sports ground and a campsite, Camping Paradis, all on your right. There is a road beside the towpath with openings where you can join it from time to time. Note that there is a road east, Route du Magnolias, which leads to a supermarket 200m away. Pass under Pont du Rat and then Pont Autoroute (PK 2,475) where you pass under the **A62** motorway. The village on your left is **Lacourt-Saint-Pierre**. Come to a modern bridge of the same name, 3.5km from the start of the canal extension. There is bar/café in the village to your left (west). Pass under this bridge as the path moves through open countryside. You reach the first lock Écluse (1 bis) de Noalhac, 4.5km from the canal beginning and 28.5km from Moissac. Bis means 'again' and is used to distinguish between two houses or places with the same number. The lock house is on the opposite bank. The bridge of the same name is shortly afterwards. The next lock, Écluse (2 bis) La Mothe is just over 500m further on. The locks now follow in quick succession: Écluse (3 bis) Fisset is 424m further on. ▸ The next lock, Bretoille (4 bis) is followed by lock/bridge Écluse Mortarieu (5 bis) just 370m later. Cross the road here. The canal swings to the left. The next locks come quickly: Écluse (6 bis) La Terrasse, Écluse (7 bis) Rabastens and lock/bridge Écluse (8 bis) Verlhaguet. The path swings right after this and there is a 1.6km stretch before the next lock/bridge: Écluse (9 bis) Bordebasse.

Reach **Montauban harbour**. It has a bar and services for the boats moored there. Follow the path to the final lock that you can cycle to on the canal, Écluse (10 bis) Montauban. There is one further lock (11 bis) which opens onto the Tarn, just over 100m away which can not

Change to the north bank.

Those wishing to skip the Canal de Montech should continue towards Toulouse on the north bank (saving 24km).

Note the large cone-shaped water tower in front and to your right.

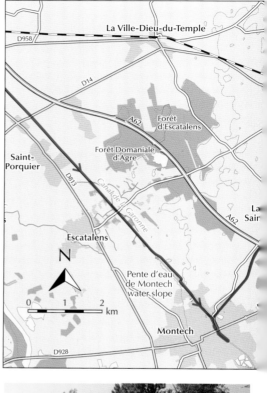

*Montauban harbour*

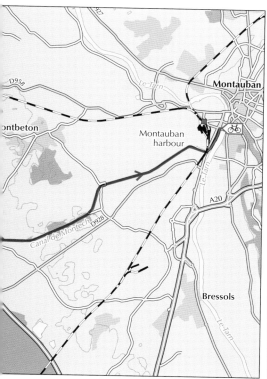

be reached by bike as the canal passes under the railway line in front of you and joins the Tarn river beside the Restaurant Club Nautique on the river. The port is 35km from Moissac.

To get to the town centre, cross the footbridge at the lock and reach the main harbour. Take the road straight in front of you, rue des Oules, with the railway track on your right and above you. Note a small dark passage on your right going underneath the railway track. ▸ Go through this – the ceiling is very low so it is best to dis-mount. Emerge onto a lane that leads to a busy road,

This passage is very easy to miss.

Avenue Marceau Hamecher (N2020). Turn right on to an unseparated cycle track and note a shop with a sign 'Alimentation' in traditional lettering on your left. This is a useful landmark when looking for the lane on your return. You see the railway tracks on your right and come to a V junction. Turn left here – it is best to cross the road at the pedestrian lights – onto an unseparated cycle track. The Tarn river is on your right as you cycle Quai Adolphe Poult although it only comes into view after a while. There is a long weir on the river where herons stand and fish. The road rises and reaches a junction with a long bridge on your right. You can cross to the centre of **Montauban** by any one of three bridges that follow: these are, in order of reaching them: Pont de Sapiac, Pont Neuf and Pont Vieux.

## MONTAUBAN

Montauban is a beautiful town. Its exquisite pink-bricked buildings reflect its importance as the capital of the Tarn et Garonne. They also mirror those that you will see in Toulouse. It is built at the confluence of the Tarn with one of its minor tributaries, the Tescou which enters the Tarn just upriver from the old bridge. The Count of Toulouse granted the town a charter in 1144. Its connection with the count meant that it was on the losing side in the Crusade against the Cathars. It was ceded to the English under the Treaty of Brétigny in 1360. The inhabitants renounced the English throne in 1414. The town sided with the Protestant forces and was the Huguenot headquarters in the 1621 uprising and as a centre for freethinking and Protestantism it opposed the Catholic King, Louis XIII. In August 1621, he laid siege to the town with a large force, reputed to be 25,000 men supported by heavy artillery. All their sorties against the town's defences were rebutted. The king decided to use a shock and awe tactic by loosing 400 cannon shots at the town at one go. They expected the townsfolk to surrender after the bombardment but in fact it appears to have increased their resistance. The siege lasted until November when illness ravaged the king's troops and they retreated. The 400 *coups* (shots) are celebrated to this day and there is a festival in early September to mark its anniversary. Cardinal Richelieu later overcame the town in 1629.

*Place Nationale*

The town is worth exploring. Its narrow streets, cafés and squares buzz with life. The Place Nationale is its centre and the place to start any visit. The buildings rise three storeys over a double arcade that surrounds the entire square. There are restaurants and cafés in the arcades and visitors can sit at tables in the main square watching the town's life pass around you. The brickwork is rose-red in colour and very similar to that found in Toulouse.

Montauban was the birthplace of the artist Jean-Auguste-Dominique Ingres (1780–1867). One of his more famous paintings, *Le Vœu de Louis XIII* (1824), adorns the Cathedral of Notre Dame (1739), while the Museum Ingres displays more of his work along with works by another Montalbanais artist Antoine Bourdelle. The museum is housed in a palace which itself was built on the site of an earlier one that the Black Prince occupied during the Hundred Years' War. This is close to the Pont Vieux, the old bridge, which dates from the 14th century.

The tourist office is housed in an old Jesuit college dating from the 17th century. One of the town's other important attractions is the church of St Jacques which dates from the 13th century. Its bell tower is octagonal in shape and there is a 19th-century mosaic above the main door.

Montauban has all the usual facilities with plenty of restaurants and hotels, etc. There is a railway station on the Bordeaux Toulouse line and most trains travelling that route stop there. A stay in the 18th-century Hotel du Commerce, in the same square as the cathedral, will add a sense of history to your visit.

## STAGE 7
### Montauban to Toulouse

| | |
|---|---|
| **Start** | Pont de Sapiac |
| **Distance** | 43km |
| **Accumulated climb** | 95m |
| **Path** | Asphalt cycle track and roads |
| **Map** | IGN TOP100 161 and 168 |
| **Detours** | Dieupendale and Verdun-sur-Garonne (6.8km); epilogue to the Garonne in Toulouse (less than 2km) |

The final stage begins by retracing your journey from Montauban to Montech before joining the main canal on the final run into Toulouse. You move from rural countryside to suburbs and then reach the city proper. There is a detour to Dieupendale and Verdun-sur-Garonne. The latter is striking with its medieval walls still intact. Its clocktower and medieval town centre are worth lingering over too. Toulouse is a bustling cosmopolitan city. The canal meets the Canal du Midi and Canal de Brienne in the Port de Bassin de L'Embouchure in the city centre. There is a short description of a cycle along the Canal de Brienne to bring you back to the Garonne allowing for a pleasing symmetry of beginning and ending with this wonderful river.

Cross the Pont de Sapiac from the old town following signs for Agen, Auch, Castelsarrasin and Gare SNCF. After 20m turn left at a junction onto Avenue Marceau Hamecher passing the *gendarmerie* on your right. Pass a left turn and shortly afterwards note the almost hidden entrance to the lane and tunnel that passes under the railway line between houses numbered 23 and 21. If you reach the shop with 'Alimentation' in old lettering above it then you have gone too far. Pass under the railway line and turn left onto rue des Oules. You reach the port in 300m. Cross the footbridge over the canal at the lock to reach the east bank. Leaving Montauban locks (10 and 11 bis) cycle back along the canal towards Montech. You pass the locks: Bordebasse (9 bis), Verlhequet (8

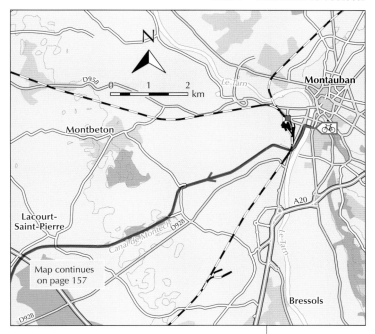

bis), Rabastens (7 bis), la Terrasse (6 bis), Mortarieu
(5 bis), Brétoille (4 bis), Fisset (3 bis) Lamothe (2 bis)

*A barge moored near
a canal house on the
Canal de Montech*

155

Should you have started your cycle in Montauban and wish to visit Montech then leave the route here and cycle back over the bridge to the town.

and Noalhac (1 bis). Continue to the junction with the Garonne canal, 12km from Montauban.

At the junction, follow the path as it swings left onto the cycle path on the north/right bank. Pass under Pont de Montech and in 500m pass the footbridge and continue on the same bank leaving Montech. ◄

Continue towards Toulouse. You quickly leave Montech's suburbs, crossing a small aqueduct. You may note open water beyond the opposite bank of the canal. This is part of a fish farm. Reach Lavache (10) lock/bridge (PK 42.032) and cross to the south side. ◄ From the lock sign, you see that you now have an 18.5km lock-free ride.

Change to south bank.

Continue on the path and 3.6km from the port at Montech you reach, Pont de Finhan (PK 39,251) which you cycle under. There is a sign to the right for the **Forêt d'Agre**.

> The 1500ha **Forêt d'Agre** area of woodland is a remnant of a much larger forest that stretched from Grenade (further south and slightly off the canal) to Castelsarrasin. It is well known for its wildlife which includes wild boar, genets, martins, foxes and a great many bird, reptile, invertebrate and plant species. In season, there are walks through the woodland as well as adventure courses for adults and children (www.agrip-aventure.fr for more details and prices).

As well as shops, a bakery and Château de Pérignon, its church tower is a national monument.

This stretch of the canal is tree-lined and very pleasant. Buzzards circle above and the trees are home to a variety of birdlife. Nearly 5km from Montech port reach another bridge, Pont de Thouret (PK 38,202) and pass under it. There is a sign for Finhan, which is 3km off route. ◄

The next bridge is the Pont de Montbartier and **Montbartier** itself is 1km away on the north bank. Pont de Bessens (PK 33,351) is 9.3km from Montech port and the village of **Bessens**, 1.5km off route, has a restaurant, bakery (1km) and a small church at its centre.

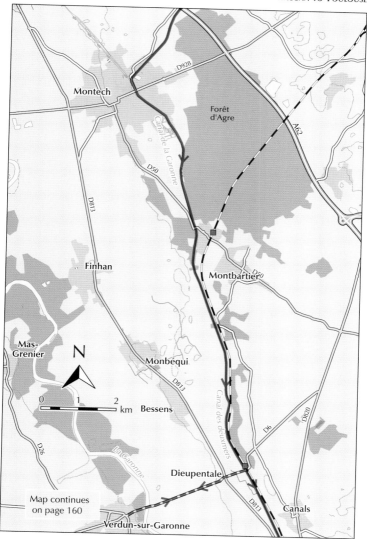

Montech

D928

Forêt
d'Agre

Canal de la Garonne

A62

D50

Finhan

Montbartier

D50

Mas-
Grenier

N

Monbéqui

D813

Canal des deux mers

0   1   2
km

D6

D820

Bessens

D26

La Garonne

Dieupentale

D813

Canals

Map continues
on page 160

Verdun-sur-Garonne

157

A medieval street in
Verdun-sur-Garonne

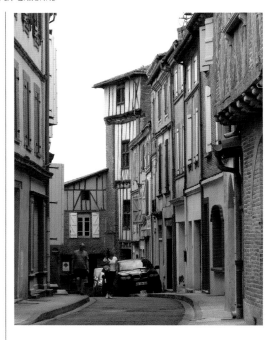

A small canal house before Pont Dieupentale (PK 31,135) now serves as a restaurant and bar in season. There are signs at the bridge for Verdun-sur-Garonne and Dieupendale.

**Detour to Dieupendale and Verdun-sur-Garonne**
From the bridge follow the sign south for both places. In 600m go straight over a roundabout following a sign for Verdun-sur-Garonne 3km. **Dieupendale**, dating back to the 10th century, is spread along the D6 on either side of the roundabout. It has a pizza restaurant, shops and a bakery.

Verdun-sur-Garonne is a further 3.8km on the D6. Note the church on your left with an interesting clock and bell tower as your leave Dieupendale. Take care on this busy, straight road before crossing an attractive, modern suspension bridge (Pont Porte-de-Gasgogne) over the Garonne and entering **Verdun-sur-Garonne**.

> **Verdun-sur-Garonne** has several beautiful buildings and monuments and, as befits its importance in medieval times, was surrounded by walls with an additional moat. The half-timbered houses along the defences add to the sense of antiquity. Its church, originally named Saint Michel, dates from 1216 and is a national monument, as is its organ. The 14th-century clocktower gate formed part of the original town walls and now stands amid the half-timbered houses. The market place is built of red brick with wooden beams and is across from the town hall. Queen Margot's castle is a private chateau in the west of the town whose tower peeps above the trees.

Return by the same route.

Pass under the Pont Dieupentale observing the signs to keep to the right. Some 700m later note the canalised Lamothe stream. A large road, the **D813**, becomes more intrusive here. Pont de Villelongue is next (PK 29,379), 1.7km from Pont Dieupentale. Trains are more frequent on the tracks on the opposite side of the canal. There is a sign warning that the path is shared with cars at the next bridge (Saint Jean) some 400m further on. You pass under the next modern bridge (Grisolles) approximately 1.3km on from the previous one. This carries the RD813 from Agen. It joins the D820 on the northern side of the bridge and continues towards Toulouse.

A further 1.2km brings you to Pont Larroque (PK 26,685). There is a sign for **Grissoles**. There are picnic tables and a tap by the bridge on the Toulouse side; the railway station is on the opposite bank.

> The small town of **Grisolles** was originally called 'Ecclesiola' or small church and was part of the

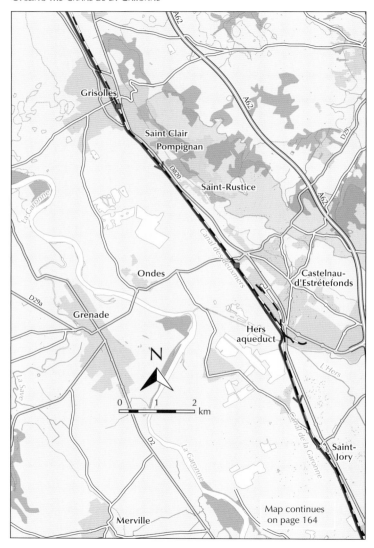

Map continues
on page 164

*The covered market in Grisolles*

Abbey of St Sernin in Toulouse. The municipal music school is beside the canal bridge. The town is home to a museum founded in 1938 by the poet and writer Theodore Calbet. The building is a converted half-timbered village house. It doubles as an exhibition space for artists exploring local themes and culture.

Saint Martin's Church is in front of the museum. The original church dated back to AD844 but it was replaced in 19th century. The metal marketplace was built between 1893 and 1894 replacing an earlier wooden structure. Its design was inspired by the work of the architect Victor Baltard the designer of Les Halles in Paris. There are shops and bakeries in the town.

Pass exercise equipment and Pont de Grisolles (PK 29.902), 700m from Grisolles. The canal is close to a main road and the railway line. Note villages on your left, **St-Clair** and **Pompignan**. The next bridge, Pont de

Pompignan (PK 24,8744), takes you to the village, just off route.

**Pompignan** has basic shops, as well as a restaurant and pizza outlet. Its mid-18th-century chateau is famed for a collection of musical instruments. Its gardens are considered one of the earliest and most extensive landscaped in France and include a number of follies as well as an extensive watering system.

Continue on a more exposed stretch to Pont de Saint Rustice (PK 23,682). The village of **Saint-Rustice** is on the opposite bank. The path is shared with cars for a time. There is a large, red-brick water mill on your right at the next lock and you cross over the mill race as you climb to the bridge at Écluse (9) de Embalens. A church and chateau perched on a hill on the northern bank come into clearer view.

The chateau of **Castelnau-d'Estrétefonds** dates from medieval times and 12th-century records refer to it. The church was built in the 16th century but you can see the preserved bell wall of the ancient (AD961) church of Saint-Martin. The town of Castelnau-d'Estrétefonds has supermarkets, other shops and restaurants. There are hotels close by serving Toulouse.

A large car depot with the cars sheltered under solar panelled sun shields is on the opposite bank as you approach lock/bridge, Écluse (8) de Castelnau. The lock has a large overflow beside it – a common feature at the following locks.

The seventh lock, Hers, is less than a kilometre away. The **Hers aqueduct** carrying the canal over the Hers river is just beyond it. There are elegant metal railings on either side. Note the red-bricked arches below supporting the aqueduct. Cross this and then pass under a bridge. The path runs beside a road and is separated from it by

wooden fence 2.5km from Hers lock. This leads to the next lock: Saint-Jory (6). There is an underpass for cyclists and pedestrians.

*Large overflows are common around locks: this one powered a mill*

> The village of **Saint-Jory**, a site for Marian devotion, is on the opposite bank. The church of Notre-Dame de Beldou was originally a pagan temple but, with the coming of Christianity, became a site of devotion to the Blessed Virgin. A spring close by is still revered by Saint-Joryens.

Cycle along the tree-lined path to Écluse (5) de Bordneuve, 2km from Saint-Jory lock. The lock house is blocked and boarded up and looks forlorn. Pass under a bridge and within 200m rise to the bridge/lock Écluse (4) Lespinasse. The town of the **Lespinasse** has the usual services except hotels. Its church dates from the 12th

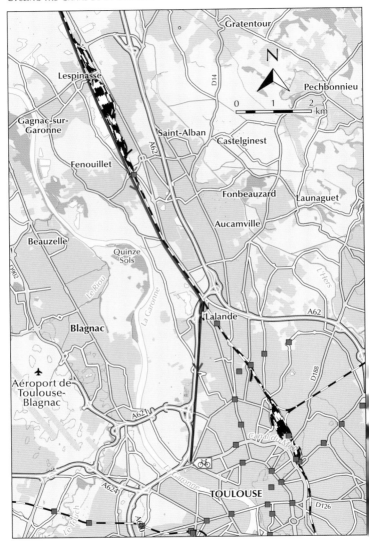

century and there are walks around the lake on your right.

Pass the church on your right as you pedal towards Toulouse with a large railway yard to your left and a body of water to your right. A cycle track right leads to Fenuoillet centre. Some 800m further on you pass under two road bridges before climbing to a bridge/lock: Écluse (3) de Fenouillet. The surrounding countryside inspired the artist Henri Matisse and two paintings of the area, *Les Gourgues* and *Maisons à Fenouillet*, are in the Matisse Museum in Nice.

The land is agricultural to the right before the next bridge/lock: Écluse (2) de Lacourtensourt. There is a sign for the campsite, Camping le Rupé, at the next bridge, 200m to the right and visible later from the path. The next bridge, 700m further on, carries the A624 motorway. Pass under this and another road bridge after 300m. Climb to the final bridge/lock on the canal, Écluse (1) de Lalande, 200m later.

Lalande town is on the canal's northern bank. It has basic services and is a dormitory town for Toulouse. There is an unusual contraption on the south bank beside a canal overflow channel. It removes and mangles weeds and debris floating in the canal – unfortunately it attracts a lot of flies.

For the final 4km to Toulouse, change to the north/right bank at Lalande. ▸ There may be a barrier preventing you from passing in front of the lock house. If so, take the road behind it and rejoin the path in 20m. There is a picnic area here. Pass a rowing club. Go under two modern bridges, 2.6km from Lalande lock. The railway and sidings are to the left while the A62 motorway is on the opposite bank. You may notice that air pollution increases as you cycle – depending on weather conditions. Asthma sufferers should take note.

The canal passes through industrial and commercial centres. There are shacks and tents on both canal banks. Pass under a motorway bridge and, 3km from Lalande lock, join a cycle path beside the canal separated from Boulevard de Genève by kerbstones. Cross a road at a

Change to north bank.

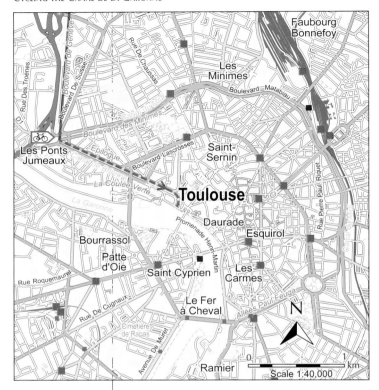

pedestrian crossing to your left and then cross the road in front of you to reach the Port de l'Embouchure, Les Ponts Jumeaux – the twinned bridges. You have reached the port where the three canals, the Garonne canal, the Canal du Midi and the Canal de Brienne, meet. The bridges are over the canals; you are in **Toulouse** proper. Look left to see the Canal du Midi which continues to the Mediterranean, while in front of you is the bridge over the Canal de Brienne which links the two canals to the Garonne river and supplies water for the Garonne canal.

## TOULOUSE

*Place du Capitole*

Toulouse is a lively, cosmopolitan city. University students keep it young and vital. Cafés are filled with conversation while its streets, squares and markets are full of life. It combines old with new. It has a rich and complex history while being a major centre for hi-tech industries such as aerospace and it is where the European Airbus has its headquarters and research and manufacturing facilities.

It is known as the 'Rose City' because of the pink/red brick used in most of its major buildings. The river Garonne was its main trading route prior to the canal's construction. Trade flourished with the canals and the city's buildings reflect the wealth created. Its modern architecture echoes its more recent success as a technological centre.

Toulouse is easy to negotiate on bike or on foot. It has a well-developed network of cycle lanes and tracks. There are dedicated cycle tracks beside roads, some counter-flow, and others are shared with bus lanes. The local authority produces a map of these downloadable from www.toulouse.fr. You can also get a copy from the tourist office. The city's public transport system is excellent. It has a metro, bus and tram system with daily and three-day passes. Its airport is close by in Blagnac while its central train station, Gare Matabiau, is beside the Canal du Midi on Boulevard Pierre Sémard. The city is worth at least a day's visit. Some of its most attractive buildings date from the 15th to the 17th century. This was the city's golden age when its merchants became wealthy from the production of the blue dye pastel, also known as woad, produced from the leaves of pastel plants. The city's streets are narrow with the tall buildings giving welcome shade. The streets' names are often given in two languages: Occitan and French. The latter are used on maps. The Garonne river is lined with walks, parks and public spaces, and south-facing cafés near the river on the right bank allow you to sit outside even in winter. The river can be viewed from any number of bridges, but the Pont Neuf offers the traditional view (and one of the best).

Most of its main attractions are within walking distance of the central square, Place du Capitole. The city hall or Capitole is the square's main building and named after the *capitouls* or consuls (rich merchant rulers). Its 128m-long facade has eight columns representing the eight consuls. Cafés and restaurants under the arches around the square are great places to sit and watch the Toulousains go by. The Saturday and Tuesday morning markets sell local and organic produce; for much of the rest of the time the square is a stage for performers and musicians.

*The Donjon*

The tourist office is located in the Donjon, a 16th-century building restored by Villet-le-Duc in the 19th century behind the Capitol. A passageway through the central arch, no longer open to the public for security reasons, has a plaque on the ground marking the spot where Henri de Montmorency was executed after his forces were defeated by the king's army at Castelnaudary.

Three of Toulouse's many churches stand out as worth visiting. Basilique Saint Sernin was built on the site of an earlier basilica housing the remains of Saint Sernin, bishop of Toulouse who was martyred in AD250 for refusing to take part in the sacrifice of a bull: he was tied to its legs and dragged down a flight of stone steps. The church, 115m long, was a major stopping point for medieval pilgrims en route to Santiago de Compostela in Spain. Key points to note are its multi-tiered bell tower, its beautiful doors and extraordinary interior.

Those interested in the Cathar religion and its persecution may wish to visit the church known as the Jacobins, the site of the first Dominican monastery, founded in 1216. The Dominicans are known as the Order of Preachers and their founder, Saint Dominic, preached against heresy and the order later spearheaded the inquisition against the Cathar faith.

The church takes its name from the order's first church in Paris, Saint Jacques, and the monks consequently became known as the Jacobins. The order built the church and Toulouse's first university. The church is red brick and a masterpiece. The interior is divided into two naves, its relative narrowness and height adding to its impact, with Saint Thomas Aquinas's sarcophagus given a central location. There is a charge to visit the cloisters but it is well worth it.

Saint Étienne cathedral is the final resting place of the Canal du Midi's creator and builder, Pierre-Paul Riquet. His vision inspired the later construction of the Garonne canal. Riquet is buried close to a pillar on the right as you enter. The main part of the cathedral was built in the 13th century and contains an impressive choir with wooden stalls. One of the early stained-glass windows dates from the 15th century and shows King Charles VII of France together with the Dauphin Louis, later to become Louis XI; there are also locally produced tapestries from 16th and 17th century.

The city has many other attractions. The Augustins Museum (21 rue de Metz) houses a collection that includes early Christian artefacts. The Georges Labit Museum (17 rue du Japon) displays items collected by Georges Labit in the 19th century and concentrates on his Asian and Egyptian collections. The Saint Raymond Museum (Place St Sernin) has displays of art and archaeology from early centuries to the Middle Ages. The Bemberg Foundation was donated to Toulouse and is a collection of paintings from the French Renaissance and the French modern school. It is housed in the Hôtel d'Assézat in Place d'Assézat. The Botanical Gardens (Jardins des Plantes) has plants from as far away as Japan. The Natural History Museum, the medical school, Saint Exupère Church and the Daniel Sorano Theatre border the gardens. The Space City Theme Park (Avenue Jean Gonord in eastern part of the city close to the A61 and 5km from the centre) displays full-sized space craft, rockets and space stations including the Soyouz space craft and an exact replica of the Mir space station.

## Epilogue

This guide began at the Garonne river. A short, less than 2km, trip along the Canal de Brienne brings you back to that river. Those wishing to complete the circle should cross the bridge over the Canal du Midi at the Port de l'Embouchure and join a rough stony path with occasional mucky patches, beside the Canal de Brienne on your right. There is a lock with a footbridge at the start of the canal. You pass through central Toulouse but you do not see a lot of it from the path. Pass under a footbridge after 500m and shortly afterwards under two stone bridges reminiscent of those in Port de l'Embouchure. You see the back of a church before you pass under the last bridge. This is the Église Saint Pierre des Cuisines, dating from the fifth century. It is built on a Roman necropolis and is a national monument. Its crypt contains archaeological remains of an earlier Christian church. The name derives from the word *coquinis* meaning craftsmen. You reach the second and final lock Écluse St Pierre which is, according to its sign, 1573m from the port. The lock gates are tall and dramatic, flanked on both sides by flights of steep stone steps. You have to climb two flights to reach the road. Turn right and cross the road in front of you, the quay de Dillon and reach the river. There is a bridge, Pont Saint Pierre, to your left and a weir to your right. A watermill, the Moulins du Bazacle, is beside the weir. In front of you is the dome of the Chapelle Saint-Joseph de la Grave. Follow the quay towards the bridge to a small busy square, Place St Pierre. This is a lively place with cafés and bars – a good place to stop and mark the end of your cycle.

If you want to cycle further, return to the port and follow the Canal du Midi as it continues the journey to the Mediterranean Sea. *Cycling the Canal du Midi*, published by Cicerone, will guide you on the way.

# APPENDIX A

*Distances between locks*

**Locks from Castets-en-Dorthe on the Garonne Canal**

| Number | Name of lock | Distance from last lock (km) | Distance to next lock (km) | Distance from start (km) |
|--------|--------------|------------------------------|----------------------------|--------------------------|
| 53 | Castets | 0.0 | 0.529 | 0.0 |
| 52 | Les Gares | 0.5 | 0.7 | 0.5 |
| 51 | Mazerac | 0.7 | 4.4 | 1.2 |
| 50 | Bassane | 4.4 | 4.1 | 5.7 |
| 49 | Fontet | 4.1 | 2.6 | 9.8 |
| 48 | l'Auriole | 2.6 | 7.5 | 12.4 |
| 47 | Gravières | 7.5 | 2.5 | 19.9 |
| 46 | des Bernes | 2.5 | 5.2 | 22.4 |
| 45 | l'Avance | 5.2 | 9.9 | 27.6 |
| 44 | du Mas | 9.9 | 5.6 | 37.5 |
| 43 | de la Gaulette | 5.6 | 2.7 | 43.1 |
| 42 | La Gaule | 2.7 | 4.7 | 45.8 |
| 41 | de Berry | 4.7 | 10.4 | 50.5 |
| 40 | de Larderet | 10.4 | 0.2 | 60.9 |
| 39 | de Bäise | 0.2 | 7.0 | 61.1 |
| 38 | de l'Auvignon | 7.0 | 14.6 | 68.1 |
| 37 | de Rosette | 14.6 | 0.4 | 82.8 |
| 36 | de Chabrières | 0.4 | 0.4 | 83.2 |
| 35 | Marianette | 0.4 | 0.4 | 83.6 |
| 34 | d'Agen | 0.4 | 12.6 | 83.9 |
| 33 | de Saint Christophe | 12.6 | 3.1 | 96.5 |
| 32 | du Noble | 3.1 | 6.9 | 99.7 |
| 31 | Lamagistère | 6.9 | 6.3 | 106.6 |
| 30 | Valence d'Agen | 6.3 | 1.9 | 113.0 |
| 29 | Pommevic | 1.9 | 1.5 | 114.8 |
| 28 | du Braguel | 1.5 | 5.7 | 116.4 |
| 27 | Petit Bezy | 5.7 | 3.8 | 122.1 |
| 26 | d'Espagnette | 3.8 | 3.6 | 125.9 |

| Number | Name of lock | Distance from last lock (km) | Distance to next lock (km) | Distance from start (km) |
|--------|--------------|------------------------------|----------------------------|--------------------------|
| 25 | Moissac | 3.6 | 0.6 | 129.5 |
| 24 | Gregonne | 0.6 | 0.6 | 130.1 |
| 23 | du Cacor | 0.6 | 2.7 | 130.7 |
| 22 | d'Artel | 2.7 | 0.5 | 133.4 |
| 21 | Verries | 0.4 | 0.5 | 133.8 |
| 20 | de St Jean des Vignes | 0.5 | 1.4 | 134.3 |
| 19 | Castelsarrasin | 1.4 | 2.3 | 135.7 |
| 18 | Prades | 2.3 | 3.4 | 137.9 |
| 17 | St Martin | 3.4 | 4.5 | 141.3 |
| 16 | Escatalens | 4.5 | 2.2 | 145.8 |
| 15 | Pommies | 2.2 | 0.6 | 148.0 |
| 14 | Escudies | 0.6 | 0.4 | 148.6 |
| 13 | Pellaborie | 0.4 | 0.4 | 149.0 |
| 12 | des Peyrets | 0.4 | 0.7 | 149.4 |
| 11 | Montech | 0.7 | 2.1 | 150.2 |
| 10 | de Lavache | 2.1 | 18.5 | 152.3 |
| 9 | de Emballens | 18.5 | 3.2 | 170.8 |
| 8 | de Castelnau | 3.2 | 0.9 | 174.0 |
| 7 | Hers | 0.9 | 3.3 | 174.8 |
| 6 | de Saint Jory | 3.3 | 1.9 | 178.1 |
| 5 | de Bordeneuve | 1.9 | 1.9 | 180.1 |
| 4 | de Lespinasse | 1.9 | 3.8 | 181.9 |
| 3 | de Fenouillet | 3.8 | 1.1 | 185.7 |
| 2 | Lacourtenscourt | 1.1 | 2.6 | 186.8 |
| 1 | Lalande | 2.6 | 3.9 | 189.4 |
| 0 | Port de l'Embouchure | 3.9 | 0.0 | 193.3 |

**Locks on Montauban canal**

| Number | Name of lock | Distance from last lock (km) | Distance to next lock (km) | Distance from start (km) |
|--------|--------------|------------------------------|----------------------------|--------------------------|
| | l'Embranchement | 0.0 | 4.5 | 0.0 |
| 1 bis | de Noalhac | 4.5 | 0.5 | 4.5 |
| 2 bis | Lamothe | 0.5 | 0.4 | 5.0 |
| 3 bis | Fisset | 0.4 | 0.8 | 5.4 |
| 4 bis | Bretoille | 0.8 | 0.4 | 6.2 |
| 5 bis | Mortarieu | 0.4 | 0.4 | 6.6 |
| 6 bis | la Terrasse | 0.4 | 0.3 | 6.9 |
| 7 bis | Rabastens | 0.3 | 0.3 | 7.3 |
| 8 bis | Verlhaguet | 0.3 | 1.6 | 7.6 |
| 9 bis | Bordebasse | 1.6 | 1.5 | 9.2 |
| 10 bis | Montauban | 1.5 | 0.1 | 10.7 |
| 11 bis | du Tarn | 0.1 | 0.0 | 10.8 |

# APPENDIX B
*Accommodation*

This is not an exhaustive list. The suggested accommodation is spaced along the canal or excursions to allow you to plan ahead. Contact details include a telephone number with the international prefix. Remove the +33 and insert a 0 to call a number from within France.

## Bordeaux

### Hotels

Intercontinental Hotel – le Grand Hotel
2–5 Place de la Comédie
tel +33 5573044
www.intercontinental.com/bordeaux

Hôtel Mercure Bordeaux Saint-Jean
28–30 rue de Tauzia
tel +33 556922121
www.mercure.com

Hôtel Novotel Bordeaux Centre
45 cours du Maréchal Juin
tel +33 556514646
www.novotel.com

Hôtel de la Tour Intendance
14–16 rue de la Vieille Tour
tel +33 556445656
www.hotel-tour-intendance.com

Hôtel California
22 rue Charles Domercq
tel +33 556911725
www.hotelcalifornia-bordeaux.com

Hôtel de France
7 rue Franklin
tel +33 556482411
www.hotel-france-bordeaux.fr

### Chambres d'hôtes

Arène Bordeaux
29 rue Emile Fourcand
tel +33 616064831
larenebordeaux@gmail.com

Une Chambre en Ville
25 rue Bouffard
tel +33 556813453
www.une-chambre-en-ville-bordeaux.com

La Course
69 rue de la Course
tel +33 556522807
contact@lacourse-bordeaux.fr

Villa Bordeaux
48 bis cours de la Somme
tel +33 556317727
www.bordeauxchambresdhotes.com

### Camping

Boulevard Jacques Chaban-Delmas
Nouveau Stade de Bordeaux
33520 Bruges
tel +33 557877060
www.camping-bordeaux.com

**Prologue: Bordeaux to Lacanau Océan**

**St Médard-en-Jalles**

*Hotels*
Hotel Ibis Styles
1 Avenue de la Boétie
33160 Saint-Médard-en-Jalles
tel +33 556991111
www.accorhotels.com

**Salaunes**

*Chambres d'Hotes*
Maggy Degardin
18 Chemin de la Gravette
33160 Salaunesmob +33 699388907
tel +33 556568609
www.lesruchesdesalaunes.fr

Domaine du Plec
Hervé Villemonte de la Clergerie
1 Chemin de la Gravette
33160 Salaunes
mob +33 689898446
(camping, mobile home and yurt hire
also a possibility)

**Sainte Hélène**

*Chambres d'hôtes*
La Forestière
93 Route De Bordeaux
33480 Sainte-Hélène
tel +33 609812798
Catherinegay33@gmail.com

**Le Moutchic**

*Hotels*
Hôtel Restaurant Le Moutchico
64 Avenue de la Plage
33680 Lacanau
tel +33 556030005
www.moutchico.fr

*Camping*
Camping le Tedey
Route de Longarisse
33680 Lacanau
tel +33 556030015
www.le-tedey.com

L'Ermitage Camping-Nature
Chemin de l'Hermitage – Le Moutchic
33680 Lacanau
tel +33 556030024
www.ermitage-lacanau.com

**Lacanau Océan**

*Hotels*
Hôtel Côte d'Argent
3, Boulevard de la Plage
33680 Lacanau Océan
tel +33 556032158
www.hotel-lacanau.fr

Best Western Golf Hotel
Domaine de l'Ardilouse
33680 Lacanau Océan
tel +33 5560 9292
www.golf-hotel-lacanau.fr

Vitalparc
Route du Baganais
33680 Lacanau Océan
tel +33 556039100
www.vitalparc.com

**Stage 1: Bordeaux to
Sauveterre-de-Guyenne**

**Latresne**

*Hotels*
Hotel d'Arcins
11 Bis Avenue de la Libération
33360 Latresne
tel +33 556201527
www.hotel-arcins.fr

## Sadirac

*Chambres d'hôtes*
Le Velo Vert
30 chemin de Darrigault
33670 Sadirac
tel +33 556306326
www.chambres-hotes-velovert.com

*Camping*
Camping Bel-Air
150 Route Départementale 671
Sadirac
33670 Créon
www.camping-bel-air.com

## Créon

*Hotels*
Hotel Atena
55 avenue de l'entre deux mers
33670 Créon
tel +33 557344535
www.hotelatena.fr

Château Camiac
Route de la Forêt
33670 Créon
tel +33 556232085

## Sauveterre-de-Guyenne

*Hotels*
Bar Hôtel Restaurant de Guyenne
1 rte de Libourne Pringis
33540 Sauveterre-de-Guyenne
tel +33 556715492
www.hotel-restaurant-sauveterre.fr

*Chambres d'hôtes*
Moulin de St Léger
33540 Sauveterre-de-Guyenne
tel+33 556715994
mob +33 628377418
www.moulindestleger.com

## Stage 2: Sauveterre-de-Guyenne to Marmande

## Gabouriaud

*Chambres d'hôtes*
La Lézardière
Françoise Boehm and Rolland Chopard-Lallier
33540 Saint Martin de Lerm
tel +33 556713012
lalezardiere33@orange.fr

## La Réole

*Chambres d'hôtes*
Capu'Inn
8 Rue Bellot des Minières
33190 La Réole
tel +33 556712649
www.chambresdhotescapucinn.jimdo.com

Arts et Remparts
10 Rue Numa Ducros
33190 La Réole
tel +33 556714059
www.arts-et-remparts.com

Les Galantes
4 rue Bellot des Minières
33190 La Réole
tel +3390)556713241
mob 06 70 54 83 82
www.les-galantes.com

*Camping*
Camping du Rouergue
Lieu-dit Le Rouergue
33190 La Réole
tel +33 620319812
campinglerouergue@lareole.fr

### Mazerac

*Chambres d'hôtes*
L'Esprit Canal
26 Mazerac
33210 Castets-en-Dorthe
tel +33 651269309
www.lespritcanal.com

### Fontet

*Chambres d'hôtes*
Au Bord du Canal
22 Le Bourg Nord
Rue de l'Église
33190 Fontet
tel +33 632206629
mob +33(09)83407074
michel.prevost48@gmail.com

### Meilhan-sur-Garonne

*Hotels*
L'Auberge Meilhannaise
1, rue des Anciens Combattants
47 180 Meilhan-sur-Garonne
tel +33 61678868
www.aubergemeilhannaise.com

*Camping*
Camping Municipal au Jardin
47180 Meilhan-sur-Garonne
tel +33 553943004

### Marmande

*Hotels*
Auberge du Lion d'Or
1 rue de la République,
47200 Marmande
tel +33 553642130
www.hotelmarmande.fr

Hotel la Couronne
2 place de la Couronne
47200 Marmande
tel +33 553845431
www.hotellacouronne47.com

Hotel Restaurant Campanile Marmande
Avenue François Mitterrand D813 (3km
from centre)
47200 Marmande
tel +33 553943980
www.campanile.com/en/hotels/
campanile-marmande

### Stage 3: Marmande to Buzet-sur-Baïse

### Mas-d'Agenais

Le Dormeur du Val
Place du Marché
47430 Le Mas-d'Agenais
tel +33 553887971
www.bb-ledormeurduval.com

Relais du Mas-d'Argenais1 Rue
Labarthe47430 Le Mas-d'Agenaistel
+33 553848259
www.relaisdumasdagenais.fr

### Domaine de Méroc

Méroc (4km from centre)
47430 Le Mas-d'Agenais
tel +33 553840602

### Tonneins

*Hotels*
Le Relais des Mylandes
36 Cours de l'Yser
47400 Tonneins
tel +33 658045702
www.hotel-quai36-tonneins.com

Hôtel des Fleurs
66 Rue Colisson
47400 Tonneins
tel +33 553791047
www.hoteldesfleurs47.fr

## Damazan

*Hotels*
Inter-Hotel de la Confluence
Avenue de la Confluence
47160 Damazan
tel +33 553203828
www.hotel-damazan-agen.com

*Chambres d'hôtes*
Le Domaine du Balous
1 Rue du 19 Mars 1962
47160 Damazan
tel +33 553794296
www.domainedebalous.fr

*Camping*
Camping du lac
47160 Saint-Pierre-de-Buzet
tel +33 553897436
www.campingdulac47.com

## Saint-Léger

*Chambres d'hôtes*
Château de Grenier
47160 Saint-Léger
tel +33 553795906
www.chateaudegrenier.com

## Aiguillon

*Chambres d'hôtes*
Clos Muneau
28 Rue Victor-Hugo
47190 Aiguillon
tel +33 663245375
www.closmuneau.fr

*Camping*
Le Vieux Moulin
Route de Villeneuve
47190 Aiguillon
tel +33 553796012 (town hall)
www.ville-aiguillon.eu

## Buzet-sur-Baïsse

*Chambres d'hôtes*
Domaine de Baïse
47230 Feugarolles
tel +33 553475640
www.le-domaine-de-la-baiise.com

### Stage 4: Buzet-sur-Baïse to Agen

### St Laurent

*Chambre d'hôtes/camping*
Le Moulin St Laurent
Le Moulin
47130 Saint-Laurent
tel +33 553952408
www.moulindesaintlaurent.com

### Sérignac-sur-Garonne

*Hotel*
Hôtel le Prince Noir
6 Rue de Menjoulan
47310 Sérignac-sur-Garonne
tel +33 553687430
www.logishotels.com

*Chambre d'hôtes*
Clos de Tillet
47310 Sérignac sur Garonne
tel +33 553686345

### Moulin de St Léger

Moulin de Saint Léger de Vignague
33540 Sauveterre-de-Guyenne
tel +33 556715994
www.moulindestleger.com

## Nérac

*Hotels*
Hôtel Henri IV
4 Place du Général Leclerc
47600 Nérac
tel +33 553650063
www.hotelhenriiv.fr

Hotel-Restaurant Les Terrasses du Petit Nérac
7 Rue Séderie47600 Nérac
tel +33 553970291
www.terrasses-nerac.fr

*Chambres d'hôtes*
La Tour De Brazalem
3 Rue de l'École
47600 Nérac
tel +33 682398062
www.latourdebrazalem.fr

Domaine du Cauzeà Cause
47600 Nérac
tel +33 553655444
www.domaineducauze.fr

Moulin de Bapaumes
Lieu dit Bapomme
47600 Nérac
tel +33 785561 39
www.moulindebapaumes.com

## Agen

*Hotels*
Hôtel-Château des Jacobins
1 Place des Jacobins
2 rue Maurice Jacob
47000 Agen
tel +33 553470331
www.chateau-des-jacobins.com

Ibis Agen Centre
16 rue Camille Desmoulins
47000 Agen
tel +33 553474343
www.ibis.com

Hotel le Provence
22 cours du 14 Juillet
47000 Agen
tel +33 553473911
www.leprovence-hotel.com

Hôtel le Perigord
42 cours du 14 Juillet
47000 Agen
tel +33 553775577
www.leperigord47.fr

*Chambres d'hôtes*
Le Jardin d'Elen
12 rue Trénac
47000 Agen
tel +33 684571187
h.reveillon@laposte.net

Côté Jardin
86 rue Barleté
47000 Agen
tel +33 553964976
phillippe.rosson@neuf.fr

La Chambre d'hôtes l'Agenaise
3 impasse des Castors
47000 Agen
tel +33 553662783
joelle.fauvel@wanadoo.fr

**Stage 5: Agen to Moissac**

**Boé**

*Hotels*
Château Saint Marcel
RD813 Route de Toulouse
47550 Boé
tel +33 553871780
www.chateau-st-marcel.com

*Camping*
Parc du Château d'Allot (chalet hire)
Route de Layrac
47550 Boé
tel +33 553683311
www.domaine-dallot.fr

## Bon-Encontre

*Hotels*
Hôtel-Restaurant La Table d'Antan
41 rue de la République
47240 Bon-Encontre
tel +33 553779700
www.table-d-antan-hotel.fr

## Castelculier

*Hotels*
Akena City Agen-Castelculier
100 route du Canal
47240 Castelculier
tel +33 553692480
www.hotels-akena.com

Hôtel Balladins Agen-Castelculier
17 Chemin des Cèdres
47240 Castelculier
tel +33 553687878
www.balladins.com/en/mon-hotel/
agen-castelculier

## Saint-Jean-de-Thurac

*Chambres d'hôtes*
La Poule à Vélo
Maison éclusière 33
Écluse Saint-Christophe
47270 St-Jean-de-Thurac
tel +33 553684117
www.lapouleavelo.fr

## Valence d'Agen

*Hotels*
Hôtel le Tout Va Bien
30 place Sylvain Dumon
82400 Valence-d'Agen
tel +33 563390926
www.hotel-letoutvabien.fr

*Chambres d'hôtes*
L'Oustalet D'Anicette
33 rue Jean Capgras
82400 Valence d'Agen
tel +33 563940875
www.anicette.com

L'Escale entre 2 mers
29 rue François Moulenq
82400 Valence d'Agen
tel +33 618772934
www.lescaleentre2mers.fr

*Camping*
Camping Municipal du Val-de-Garonne
Route des Charretiers
82400 Valence d'Agen
tel +33 563398807
www.valencedagen.fr (select 'loisirs')

## Auvillar

*Hotels*
Hotel de l'Horloge
2 Place de l'Horloge
82340 Auvillar
tel +33 563399161
www.hoteldelhorlogeauvillar.com

*Chambres d'hôtes*
Château de Lastours
3 Route d'Espalais
82400 Espalais
tel +33 667534199
www.chateaudelastours.eu

**Saint-Nicolas-de-la-Grave**

*Chambres d'hotes*
Chambres d'hôtes au Château
1 Boulevard des Fossés de Raoul
82210 Saint-Nicolas-de-la-Grave
tel +33 563959682
www.au-chateau-stn.com

L'Oustal d'Adèle
740 Chemin des Arènes
82210 Saint-Nicolas-de-la-Grave
tel +33 563321276
www.gite-oustal-adele.fr

Les Glycines
Chemin de Malause
82210 Saint-Nicolas-de-la-Grave
tel +33 563946597

*Camping*
Camping Le Plan D'eau
Avenue du Plan d'Eau
82210 Saint-Nicolas-de-la-Grave
tel +33 563955002

**Moissac**

*Hotels*
Hôtel Le Moulin de Moissac
1 Promenade Sancert
82200 Moissac
tel +33 563328888
www.lemoulindemoissac.com

Le Pont Napoléon
2, allée Montébello
82200 Moissac
tel +33 563040155
www.le-pont-napoleon.com

Hôtel le Luxembourg
2 Avenue Pierre Chabrié
82200 Moissac
tel +33 563040027
www.luxembourg82.com

*Chambres d'hôtes*
La Maison du Pont St Jacques
20 Quai Magenta
82200 Moissac
tel +33 581781209
www.chambresdhotesmoissac.fr

Ultreia 45 avenue Pierre Chabrié
82200 Moissac
tel +33 563051506
www.ultreiamoissac.com

*Camping*
Le Moulin de Bidounet
Saint-Benoît
82200 Moissac
tel +33 563325252
www.camping-moissac.com

**Stage 6: Moissac to Montauban**

**Castelsarrasin**

*Hotels*
Hôtel Absolu
11 Promenade du Château
82100 Castelsarrasin
tel +33 563953323
www.hotelabsolu.fr

Hôtel Marceillac
54 Rue de l'Égalité
82100 Castelsarrasin
tel +33 563323010
www.hotelmarceillac.com

*Chambres d'hôtes*
Aux Berges du Merdaillou
1068 Chemin de Courbieu
82100 Castelsarrasin
tel +33 563324169
www.auxbergesdumerdaillou.fr

## Montech

*Camping*
Camping de Montech
520 Chemin de la Pierre
82700 Montech
tel +33 563311 29
www.camping-montech.fr

## Montauban

*Hotels*
Hôtel du Commerce
9 Place Franklin Roosevelt
82000 Montauban
tel +33 563663132
www.hotel-commerce-montauban.com

Hôtel Abbaye des Capucins
6–8 Quai de Verdun
82000 Montauban
tel +33 563220000
www.hotel-montauban-restaurant-spa-
reunion.com

Hotel Mercure
12 Rue Notre Dame
82000 Montauban
tel +33 563631723
www.accorhotels.com

Hotel Villenouvelle
30 Rue Léon Cladel
82000 Montauban
tel +33 563931 00
www.hotel.villenouvelle.fr

## Stage 7: Montauban to Toulouse

## Grisolles

*Hotels*
Logis Relais des Garrigues
Route de Fronton (D820)
82170 Grisolles
tel +33 563673159
www.relaisdesgarrigues.fr

*Camping*
Camping Aquitaine
82470 Chemin Campemengard
D 82082170 Grisolles
tel +33 563673322
www.camping-aquitaine82.com

## Saint-Jory

*Hotels*
Hôtel Restaurant Chez Mauriès
2 C Chemin Ladoux – RD 82031790
Saint-Jory
tel +33 561355224

*Chambres d'hôtes*
Au Clos Saint Georges
12 bis chemin Ladoux
31790 Saint-Jory
tel +33 561357440
www.auclossaintgeorges.com

## Toulouse

*Hotels*
Hotel Ibis Budget Toulouse Centre Gare
27 Boulevard des Minimes
31200 Toulouse
tel +33 892683110
www.accorhotels.com

Hotel Ibis Gare Matabiau
14 Boulevard Bonrepos
31000 Toulouse
tel +33 561625090
www.accorhotels.com

Hotel Ibis Ponts Jumeaux
99 Boulevard de la Marquette
3100 Toulouse
tel +33 562272828
www.accorhotels.com

The accorhotels website lists over 30 more hotels in the Toulouse area.

Hotel Kyriad Toulouse Centre
5 Boulevard de la Gare
31500 Toulouse
tel +33 561341171
www.kyriad.com

Hotel B&B Toulouse Cenre
77 Boulevard de l'Embouchure
31200 Toulouse
tel +33 298337529
www.hotel-bb.com

Hotel Icare
11 Boulevard Bonrepos
31000 Toulouse
tel +33 561636655
www.hotelicare.com

Hotel Riquet
92 Rue Riquet
31000 Toulouse
tel +33 561625596
www.hotelriquet.com

Hotel Albert 1er
8 Rue Rivals
31000 Toulouse
tel+33 561211791
www.albert1.com

*Camping*
Camping de la Bouriette
199 chemin de Tournefeuille
31300 Toulouse
tel +33 561496446
www.camping-la-bouriette-toulouse.fr

Camping le Rupé
21 Chemin du Pont de Rupé
31200 Toulouse
tel +33 561700735
campinglerupe31@wanadoo.fr

Bordeaux
Office de Tourisme et des Congrès de Bordeaux Métropole
12 Cours du 30 Juillet,
33000 Bordeaux
tel +33 556006600
www.bordeaux-tourisme.com

# APPENDIX C
## *Useful information*

### Tourist information offices

Most of the towns and villages have a tourist office. Opening hours vary, and most are closed outside the main holiday season.

The French tourist office has a website: www.france.fr. The Voie Navigables de France (VNF) (the French canal company) also has a website: www.vnf.fr.

Bordeaux
Office de TourismeGare de Bordeaux –
Saint Jean
Rue Charles Domercq, 33800
tel +33 556006600

Lacanau Ocean
Tourist Office Médoc Atlantic
Place de l'Europe,
33680 Lacanau Ocean
tel +33 556032101
www.medoc-atlantique.com

Sauveterre-de-Guyenne
Office de Tourisme
Place de la République,
33540 Sauveterre-de-Guyenne
tel +33 556715345
www.entredeuxmers.com

La Réole
Bureau de Tourisme
52 Rue André Bénac
33190 La Réole
tel +33 556611355
www.entredeuxmers.com

Marmande
Office de Tourisme du Val Garonne
11 Rue Toupinerie
47200 Marmande
tel +33 553644444
www.valdegaronne.com

Tonneins
Office de Tourisme du Val de Garonne
3 Boulevard Charles de Gaulle
47400 Tonneins
tel +33 553792279
www.valdegaronne.com

Nérac
Office de Tourisme de l'Albret
7 Avenue Mondenard
47600 Nérac
tel +33 553652775
https://albret-tourisme.com

Serignac-sur-Garonne
Office de Tourisme
7 Porte du Lau
47310 Serignac-sur-Garonne
tel +33 553683000
www.agenofficedetourisme.fr

Agen
Destination Agen
38 Rue Garonne
47000 Agen
tel +33 553473609
www.agenofficedetourisme.fr

Valence d'Agen
Office de Tourisme
27 Rue de la République
82400 Valence d'Agen
tel +33 563336167

Moissac
Office de Tourisme de Moissac
6 Place Durand de Bredon
82200 Moissac
tel +33 563040185
www.tourisme.moissac.fr

Montech
Communauté de Communes Garonne
et Canal
8 rue de la Mouscane
82700 Montech
tel +33 563275716
www.cc-garonne-canal.fr

Montauban
Office de Tourisme
4 rue du Collège
Esplanade des Fontaines - BP 201
82002 Montauban Cedex
tel +33 563636060
www.montauban-tourisme.com

Toulouse
Office de Tourisme Métropole
Donjon du Capitole
Square Charles de Gaulle – BP8001
31080 Toulouse Cedex 6
tel +33 540131531
www.toulouse.fr

**Bike repair shops**

There are bike repair shops in most of the major towns along the route. Contact the local tourist office for more details. Those along the route include:
Bordo Velo
Réparation Vente
46 quai Richelieu
33000 Bordeaux
tel +33 556309145
www.bordovelo.fr

Cool Bike
77 Quai des Chartrons
33300 Bordeaux
tel +33 533481386
www.coolbik2.wixsite.com/bordeaux

Locacycle
11 avenue Lacanau Océan
33680 Lacanau
tel +33 556263099
www.locacyclelacanau.fr

Evasion Cycles
Le Moulin Bourg
Route du Pout
33670 Créon
tel +33 984245533
www.evasioncycles.com

Les cycles du Canal
4 bis, rue Grossolle
33210 Castets-en-Dorthe
tel +33 55620581 and +33 695632080
www.lescyclesducanal.com

Sinsou Didier
50 Avenue Charles Boisvert
47200 Marmande
tel +33 553642629
www.etsdidiersinsou.sitew.fr

Decathlon Marmande
18 Avenue Hubert Ruffe
47200 Marmande
tel +33 553648250
www.decathlon.fr/fr/magasin

Retureau Pascal
2 cours Alsace-et-Lorraine
47190 Aiguillon
tel +33 553796226

Veloland
18–20 avenue du Général de Gaulle
47000 Agen
tel +33 553477676
www.veloland.com

Decathlon Agen/Boé
Zone d´Activités Commerciales de
Gardès
47550 Boé
tel +33 553985566
www.decathlon.fr/fr/magasin

EXPER'CYCLE Feutrier
736 Chemin de la Chaumière
82100 Castelsarrasin
tel + 33 974562493
www.expercycle-feutrier.fr

Guionnet Cyclosport
Zi Albasud, 87, Av d'Irlande
82000 Montauban
tel +33 563663232

Montau'Bikes
426 Avenue de Toulouse
82000 Montauban
tel +33 953294287
www.montaubikes.fr

Cycle Marc
15 Allée François Verdier
31000 Toulouse
tel +33 562260450
www.cyclesmarc.e-monsite.com

Louis et Cie
13 Allée Paul Feuga
31000 Toulouse
tel +33 562267939

Louis et Cie
46 Rue de la chaussée
31000 Toulouse
tel +33 561520158
www.lious-et-cie.com

# APPENDIX D

*English–French glossary*

| English | French |
|---|---|
| *hello* | bonjour |
| *good evening* | bonsoir |
| *goodbye* | au revoir |
| *yes* | oui |
| *no* | non |
| *please* | s'il vous plait |
| *thank you* | merci |
| *I understand* | je comprends |
| *I do not understand* | je ne comprends pas |
| *I know* | je sais |
| *I don't know* | je ne sais pas |
| *I don't speak french* | je ne parle pas français |
| *do you speak english* | parlez vous anglais? |
| *watch out* | attention! |
| *help* | aidez moi |
| *I'm lost* | je suis perdu |
| *I'm sick* | je suis malade |
| *where is…* | où est… |
| *toilet* | toilette |
| *do you have a room?* | avez-vous une chambre? |
| *with a shower/bathroom* | avec douche/sale de bains |
| *single bed* | un lit pour une personne |
| *double bed* | un grand lit |
| *dish of the day* | plat du jour |
| *meal* | le repas |
| *meat* | la viande |
| *fish* | le poisson |
| *vegetarian* | vegetarian |

| English | French |
|---|---|
| *water* | l'eau |
| *wine (white/red)* | vin (blanc/rouge) |
| *glass* | le verre |
| *tea* | thé |
| *coffee* | café |
| *with milk* | au lait |
| *turn left/right* | tournez à gauche/droit |
| *straight on* | tout droit |
| *mill* | moulin |
| *church* | église |
| *lake* | etang, lac |
| *towpath* | le chemin de halage |
| *cycle track* | la piste cyclable |
| *bicycle* | bicyclette, vélo |
| *brakes* | les freins |
| *lock* | l'antivol |
| *chain* | chaîne |
| *gears* | les vitesses |
| *wheel* | la roue |
| *tyre* | le pneu |
| *puncture* | crevaison |
| *inner tube* | la chambre à l'air |
| *broken* | cassé |
| *handlebars* | le guidon |
| *gloves* | les gants |
| *spokes* | les rayons |
| *falling branches* | chutes de branches |
| *good luck!* | bon courage! |
| *safe journey!* | bonne route! |

# APPENDIX E
*Further reading*

*Plantagenet England 1225–1360* by Michael Prestwich (Oxford University Press, 2007)

*The Song of the Cathar Wars: A History of the Albigensian Crusade* edited by Janet Shirley (Routledge, 2017)

*The History of the Albigensian Crusade, Historia Albigensis* by Peter of les Vaux-de-Cernay, translated by WA Sibly and MD Sibly (The Boydell Press, 2002)

*Guide Fluvial l'Estuaire de la Gironde* (Éditions du Breil, regularly updated)

*Guide Fluvial Aquitaine* (Éditions du Breil, regularly updated)

*Le Canal de Garonne, Quand les hommes relient les mers: Collection Mémoire et Patrimoine* by Jacques Dubourg (Les Dossiers d'Aquitaine, 2013)

*Lacanau-Océan a cents ans 1906–2006* by René Magnon (Ville Lacanau, 2006)

*Game of Spies: The Secret Agent, the Traitor and the Nazi, Bordeaux 1942–1944* by Paddy Asdown (William Collins, 2017)

*A Brilliant Little Operation: The Cockleshell Heroes and the Most Courageous Raid of World War II* by Paddy Ashdown (Aurum Press, 2012)

*Death in Bordeaux* by Allen Massie (Quartet Books, 2010)

*Dark Summer in Bordeaux* by Allen Massie (Quartet Books, 2012)

*Cold Winter in Bordeaux* by Allen Massie (Quartet Books, 2014)

*End Games in Bordeaux* by Allen Massie (Quartet Books, 2015)

# LISTING OF CICERONE GUIDES

## DERBYSHIRE, PEAK DISTRICT AND MIDLANDS

Cycling in the Peak District
Dark Peak Walks
Scrambles in the Dark Peak
Walking in Derbyshire
White Peak Walks:
    The Northern Dales
White Peak Walks:
    The Southern Dales

## SOUTHERN ENGLAND

20 Classic Sportive Rides
    in South East England
20 Classic Sportive Rides
    in South West England
Cycling in the Cotswolds
Mountain Biking on the
    North Downs
Mountain Biking on the
    South Downs
North Downs Way Map Booklet
South West Coast Path Map Booklet
    – Vols 1–3
Suffolk Coast and Heath Walks
The Cotswold Way
The Cotswold Way Map Booklet
The Great Stones Way
The Kennet and Avon Canal
The Lea Valley Walk
The North Downs Way
The Peddars Way and Norfolk
    Coast Path
The Pilgrims' Way
The Ridgeway Map Booklet
The Ridgeway National Trail
The South Downs Way
The South Downs Way
    Map Booklet
The South West Coast Path
The Thames Path
The Thames Path Map Booklet
The Two Moors Way
Walking Hampshire's Test Way
Walking in Cornwall
Walking in Essex
Walking in Kent
Walking in London
Walking in Norfolk
Walking in Sussex
Walking in the Chilterns
Walking in the Cotswolds
Walking in the Isles of Scilly
Walking in the New Forest
Walking in the North
    Wessex Downs
Walking in the Thames Valley
Walking on Dartmoor
Walking on Guernsey
Walking on Jersey

Walking on the Isle of Wight
Walking the Jurassic Coast
Walks in the South Downs
    National Park

## BRITISH ISLES CHALLENGES, COLLECTIONS AND ACTIVITIES

The Book of the Bivvy
The Book of the Bothy
The C2C Cycle Route
The End to End Cycle Route
The Mountains of England and
    Wales: Vol 1 Wales
The Mountains of England and
    Wales: Vol 2 England
The National Trails
The UK's County Tops
Three Peaks, Ten Tors

## ALPS CROSS-BORDER ROUTES

100 Hut Walks in the Alps
Across the Eastern Alps: E5
Alpine Ski Mountaineering Vol 1 –
    Western Alps
Alpine Ski Mountaineering Vol 2 –
    Central and Eastern Alps
Chamonix to Zermatt
The Karnischer Hohenweg
The Tour of the Bernina
Tour of Mont Blanc
Tour of Monte Rosa
Tour of the Matterhorn
Trail Running – Chamonix and the
    Mont Blanc region
Trekking in the Alps
Trekking in the Silvretta and
    Rätikon Alps
Trekking Munich to Venice
Walking in the Alps

## PYRENEES AND FRANCE/SPAIN CROSS-BORDER ROUTES

The GR10 Trail
The GR11 Trail
The Pyrenean Haute Route
The Pyrenees
The Way of St James – Spain
Walks and Climbs in the Pyrenees

## AUSTRIA

Innsbruck Mountain Adventures
The Adlerweg
Trekking in Austria's Hohe Tauern
Trekking in the Stubai Alps
Trekking in the Zillertal Alps
Walking in Austria

## SWITZERLAND

Cycle Touring in Switzerland
The Swiss Alpine Pass Route –
    Via Alpina Route 1

The Swiss Alps
Tour of the Jungfrau Region
Walking in the Bernese Oberland
Walking in the Valais
Walks in the Engadine –
    Switzerland

## FRANCE

Chamonix Mountain Adventures
Cycle Touring in France
Cycling London to Paris
Cycling the Canal du Midi
Écrins National Park
Mont Blanc Walks
Mountain Adventures in the
    Maurienne
The GR20 Corsica
The GR5 Trail
The GR5 Trail – Vosges and Jura
The Grand Traverse of the
    Massif Central
The Loire Cycle Route
The Moselle Cycle Route
The River Rhone Cycle Route
The Robert Louis Stevenson Trail
The Way of St James – Le Puy to
    the Pyrenees
Tour of the Oisans: The GR54
Tour of the Queyras
Vanoise Ski Touring
Via Ferratas of the French Alps
Walking in Corsica
Walking in Provence – East
Walking in Provence – West
Walking in the Auvergne
Walking in the Briançonnais
Walking in the Cevennes
Walking in the Dordogne
Walking in the Haute Savoie: North
Walking in the Haute Savoie: South
Walks in the Cathar Region

## GERMANY

Hiking and Biking in the
    Black Forest
The Danube Cycleway Volume 1
The Rhine Cycle Route
The Westweg
Walking in the Bavarian Alps

## ICELAND AND GREENLAND

Walking and Trekking in Iceland

## IRELAND

The Irish Coast to Coast Walk
The Mountains of Ireland
The Wild Atlantic Way and
    Western Ireland

For full information on all our
guides, books and eBooks,
visit our website:
**www.cicerone.co.uk**

## Walking – Trekking – Mountaineering – Climbing – Cycling

**Over 40 years, Cicerone have built up an outstanding collection of over 300 guides, inspiring all sorts of amazing adventures.**

Every guide comes from extensive exploration and research by our expert authors, all with a passion for their subjects. They are frequently praised, endorsed and used by clubs, instructors and outdoor organisations.

All our titles can now be bought as **e-books**, **ePubs** and **Kindle** files and we also have an online magazine – **Cicerone Extra** – with features to help cyclists, climbers, walkers and trekkers choose their next adventure, at home or abroad.

Our website shows any **new information** we've had in since a book was published. Please do let us know if you find anything has changed, so that we can publish the latest details. On our **website** you'll also find great ideas and lots of detailed information about what's inside every guide and you can buy **individual routes** from many of them online.

It's easy to keep in touch with what's going on at Cicerone by getting our monthly **free e-newsletter**, which is full of offers, competitions, up-to-date information and topical articles. You can subscribe on our home page and also follow us on **Facebook** and **Twitter** or dip into our **blog**.

**Cicerone – the very best guides for exploring the world.**

## CICERONE

Juniper House, Murley Moss, Oxenholme Road, Kendal, Cumbria  LA9 7RL
Tel: 015395 62069  info@cicerone.co.uk
www.cicerone.co.uk